PRAISE FOR *INSPIRE*

"*Inspire Integrity* is not a passive experience. It is not a pep talk or a soothing pat on the shoulder. Instead, Corey encourages readers to join him on a path of genuine introspection and self-examination, challenging preconceived notions and expectations along the way. He risks sharing personal experiences—some painful, some funny and some a little of both—and demonstrates that his approach actually does work for real people. The stories are real. The passion, candor and enthusiasm are real. And Corey shows a way to approach life that makes sure the rabbits we all chase are real."

— **Albert Kovacs**, Corporate Lawyer & Professor

"*Inspire Integrity* takes on the most important challenge for people today— exploring questions of purpose and meaning, and finding their life calling. Ciocchetti's engaging commentary on the life lessons he has learned in his personal and professional journey will ring true to ambitious, thoughtful people. This is an accessible guidebook for twenty-something—for ALL of us really— who are seeking to lead purpose-driven, ethical lives."

— **Jo Calhoun**, former Assistant Provost
for Academic Resources, University of Denver

"Professor Ciocchetti's unique formula for chasing real rabbits will resonate loudly with his readers, not only because of the importance of his message, but because of his style of delivery. Anyone can offer happy platitudes, but it takes a gifted writer like Ciocchetti to speak the language of young people, and, at the same time, convey important lessons that many fail to learn, even in adulthood."

— **Jill Miller**, Assistant Dean for Student Services at
the Frank Batten School of Leadership and Public Policy

Inspire Integrity

INSPIRE
INTEGRITY

CHASE AN AUTHENTIC LIFE

COREY CIOCCHETTI

NEW YORK

LONDON • NASHVILLE • MELBOURNE • VANCOUVER

INSPIRE INTEGRITY

Chase an Authentic Life

Published in New York, New York, by Morgan James Publishing. Morgan James is a trademark of Morgan James, LLC. www.MorganJamesPublishing.com

The Morgan James Speakers Group can bring authors to your live event. For more information or to book an event visit The Morgan James Speakers Group at www.TheMorganJamesSpeakersGroup.com.

ISBN 9781683504399 paperback
ISBN 9781683504405 eBook
Library of Congress Control Number: 2017901734

Cover Design by:
Megan Whitney
megan@creativeninjadesigns.com

Interior Design by:
Chris Treccani
www.3dogcreative.net

In an effort to support local communities, raise awareness and funds, Morgan James Publishing donates a percentage of all book sales for the life of each book to Habitat for Humanity Peninsula and Greater Williamsburg.

Get involved today! Visit
www.MorganJamesBuilds.com

TO JILLIAN, MY LIFE

TABLE OF CONTENTS

ON CHASING RABBITS

Late into a serene summer evening, on a lofty balcony, a woman huddled with a dear friend. These heart-to-hearts were tradition and she was delighted. You see, her compatriot was a world-renowned racing greyhound named Cash. Their chat marked the eve of a lucrative race. Cash was famous for good reason. When he raced, this dog ran with all his might. He trained hard, dedicated his life to his craft and won and won. Each triumph brought royalties, distinction, and a glamorous lifestyle to the woman, his owner. She modeled prosperity. The friends recounted past successes and pondered future victories.

The conversation kicked off like always but ended quite differently. The night before the biggest race of Cash's life, the woman asked, "So, are you ready for the big day? We are a lock to win, the best in the field. This will be our largest prize. The media is all over the story and your fans will fill the stands. Records will fall as our fortunes grow. Isn't it thrilling?"

Cash replied, in an oddly sheepish, yet resolved manner, "Ummm … well. I need to say something. I don't know how to break this to you and I doubt tonight is proper. But, I am pulling myself out of tomorrow's event. In fact, I am hanging it up forever and retiring. I have run my final race."

Dumbfounded, the owner staggered, "Wait, I don't understand. Are you too old?"

Cash answered, "I still have a lot of race left in me. In fact, I'm much faster than the young pups out there."

Grasping for answers, the woman pried, "So, are you hurt?"

"It's the opposite." Cash replied. "Never felt better."

"Well." inquired the owner, increasingly frustrated, "Do I mistreat you? Are you mad at me?"

"Come on," muttered Cash, "you're my best friend. I'm lost without you."

"Then why? Why won't you race?" the woman prodded. "You're so good at this; you were born to run this fast, this gracefully. We've worked for years to get to this point – right here, the pinnacle of an astonishing career. If you retire now, we will miss out on ever growing paydays, worldwide fame, and a chance to go down as the most successful racing duo in history! Are you really willing to give up the money, glory, and fame and do something else with your life?"

To that, Cash countered, "I've been pondering my life. After some critical reflection, it dawned on me that all I have ever done is run and run around these little oval, dirt tracks. That chase sums up my life, my identity. And, I finally discovered that, after all my efforts, those little white rabbits everyone, everywhere encourages me to chase. . . they aren't even real! I choose to step aside from this race and chase things that can make me happy."[1]

---

1   This wonderful fable was adapted from a version told to me by John Bogle (founder of The Vanguard Group) during a presentation to the University of Denver's Daniels College of Business on November 1, 2006. Bogle bragged that the story was passed to him by the Reverend Fred Craddock (Professor Emeritus at Emory University's Candler School of Theology).

INTRODUCTION

LIFE'S CHALLENGE ...
TO BE HAPPY

ife presents the ultimate challenge – to be authentically happy. Authentic people possess an outer persona that reflects their inner beliefs and character. The face they present to the world mirrors who they truly are deep down.

Authentically happy people, in turn, possess and reflect contentment, gratitude, kindness, and joy. They have no need to fake happiness. They relish being around happy people and seek to persuade the rest. Essentially, their souls shine from the inside out.

Authentic happiness is that rare goal that people seek solely as an end. Our other goals are mere means to become happy. Think about it. We get married and start families because being surrounded by people to love makes us happy. We work to find fulfillment and make our communities better because leaving a legacy makes us happy. We travel because new, adventurous, and memorable experiences make us happy. We exercise to become healthy because physical fitness decreases pain, increases energy, and releases endorphins and all that makes us happy. You get the idea. You rarely witness people seek happiness so that something better or greater or grander happens. Happiness marks the end of the road, our destination.

An authentically happy life is within everyone's reach, but it can be elusive. Life is tough and the world often conspires against us. Our successes are followed by battles where magic formulas evaporate under pressure, Ten Steps to Happiness programs rarely push the right buttons or delve deep enough, and hunkering down to wait for a better opportunity consistently proves futile. These shortcuts are hardwired into our daily existence, but they prove ineffective here. Make no mistake about it, the pursuit of happiness is a constant struggle with our own nature, the world around us, and conventional wisdom. Ironically, cultivating authentic happiness is a slow, often painful process where you must persevere by gaining inches not touchdowns. This makes it a noble goal and worthy enough to be emblazoned in the most famous line of America's founding document, the Declaration of Independence. The courageous "pursuit of (authentic) happiness" is an inalienable right as valuable as our other basic human rights of life and liberty. That truth is indeed self-evident.

Sadly, authentic happiness remains out of reach for many despite our best efforts. We do not miss the mark because happiness seekers are lazy or unintelligent. The world is full of hard-working, knowledgeable folks. We do not fail due to a shortage of well-crafted plans or resources. Thousands of "secrets to happiness" lurk in the public domain and an authentically happy life comes free of charge. Finally, we do not go astray because we lack good luck, positive family influences, or role models. Happiness is available to all regardless of identity or circumstance - it does not discriminate.

Authentic happiness remains inaccessible because we fail to chase the things in life with the capacity to make a human being authentically happy. These "real rabbits" are just not sexy enough. Instead, we follow the conventional wisdom that touts money, attractiveness, and renown as bountiful happiness-producers. We read about it online and watch it on television. Popular culture misleads us and claims that these fake rabbits are our tickets to pleasure and peace of mind.

We fail to grasp that, past a certain, rather low threshold, money provides diminishing returns in terms of happiness. Wealth acquisition certainly does not produce more joy, affection, or tranquility. In the end, people adapt to their income level and it takes more and more money to increase happiness. We also fail to consider that popularity and renown might make us less happy, more introverted, less social, and perhaps even shorten our lives. Finally, we fail to realize often enough that attractiveness is incapable of providing long-term happiness and our character is what matters. Beauty truly is only skin deep. We sort of sense all this at our core but, in case a gut feeling seems untrustworthy, there is solid data backing up each of these conclusions.

The failure can be attributed to Benjamin Franklin's famous line, "Life's tragedy is that we get old too soon and wise too late." We fake-rabbit chasers eventually wise up and begin to see that our strategy is flawed. But, at that point, we are immersed in the race. We see that others appear happy with their wealth, good looks, and fame. It's difficult to swallow our pride, admit defeat, and start over. No one wants to quit. So, we chase on like Cash and eventually encounter similar results.

This book provides encouragement for you to pivot and chase real rabbits. Instead of spending time and energy focusing on money, attractiveness, and renown, you should work towards contentment, a few solid friendships, and a highly-developed character. That's it, just these three things. That is a full life, my friend. Of course, this is easier said than done. The road to happiness becomes much clearer, however, when you master a few important skills like aligning your priorities to your heart's desires and honing the ability to think, laugh at yourself, and get goose bumps every day. The goal is not to be perfect – that always backfires when humans are involved. Instead, you should seek to be intentional about the chase.

In the end, you will find that a taste of going after what matters in life is addicting. You will want more time with your family, more waking up happy, and more kindness and honesty in your daily life. You will crave the genuine respect you receive as a good person. And then, people are likely to give you the biggest compliment a person can receive: "You seem truly happy. Tell me why?"

THE REAL RABBITS CHASE … ON YOUR MARK, GET SET, GO!

We proceed in three parts modeled on a track meet. In any serious race, runners gather and are instructed to get, "On Your Mark." This is their lane, their starting place. Here, they find a stable structure where they find their footing and prepare to run straight ahead. Think of this as their foundation. If this structure is shaky, the runner will stumble out of the gate and fall behind. If this structure points in the wrong direction, the runner will soon be off track. Next, an official tells the runners to, "Get Set!" This means the race is imminent. Everyone clears their mind of all the clutter, gets in a running stance, and focuses solely on the goal – the finish line. Finally, the gun sounds, the official exclaims, "Go!" and they're off. The race has begun and the runners now rely on the skills they have practiced time and again to run quickly, efficiently, and agilely until the end.

The journey to authentic happiness begins and proceeds like a race. It requires a proper foundation of character, a mark so to speak. It requires a goal to focus on while getting set to run – a better, happier you. Moreover, it requires the running of an efficient and agile race – we only have so much time to make a difference on this Earth. Therefore, this book follows a similar sequence.

Part I – ON YOUR MARK – encourages the development of a strong moral character. This is your mark, your foundation. Dig in here as a prerequisite to authentic success and happiness. CHAPTER I demonstrates that character cannot be built solely from a lifestyle that revolves around money, good looks, or prestige. Though none of these things are bad *per se*, neither do they possess the capacity to make a person authentically happy. CHAPTER 2 demonstrates that you cannot develop strong character from ethics instruction alone. First, you must buy into and strongly pursue the idea that being a good person matters. Then, and only then, will ethics instruction have any effect. CHAPTER 3 explains how the lack of a strong character can cost you in job prospects and life more generally. Therefore, it is important to muster the courage to orient your life towards the real rabbits of contentment, relationships, and character and away from the fake rabbits of wealth, good looks, and renown. CHAPTERS 4 through 7 form the meat of this foundational part, the identification and discussion of fake rabbits. CHAPTER 5 deals with <u>Money</u>, CHAPTER 6 with <u>Beauty</u>, and CHAPTER 7 with <u>Popularity</u> and <u>Renown</u>. Overall, the goal of Part I is to evaluate these ideas through the story of a person who learned these lessons the hard way so you need not. Through this journey, we will identify our mark beyond a reasonable doubt.

Part II – GET SET – identifies and evaluates the three primary real rabbits – an authentic <u>Sense of Contentment</u>, <u>Solid Relationships</u> with a few people, and a <u>Strong Character</u>. CHAPTER 8 begins by defining contentment and then attempts to explain why 67% of Americans admit they do not wake up in such a state. We travel to rural Peru, Paris, and a Mexican fishing village to discern the true meaning of contentment. CHAPTER 9 focuses on the importance of relationships. The idea is to find three to five real friends – people who will rush into your life when others rush out – and then plug deeply into those relationships. CHAPTER 10 encourages you to focus on your character. What does it mean to be a high character person? This chapter briefly covers a few ethical decision-making frameworks to help you develop the character you need to be authentically happy. We conclude that people of high moral character act virtuously, regardless of whether someone is watching. They seek the greatest amount of happiness for themselves and others. And, they abide by a sense of duty. They do things the right way because that is what they are supposed to do and not because they want people to think they are honest, courageous, and kind.

Part III – GO – provides you with the most important tool you need to complete your race. I can say with confidence that CHAPTER 11 on <u>Priorities</u> will be the most profound thing you will read all year. That is how confident I am that you must get your priorities straight to be happy. I will show you how it's done through a simple homework assignment. There is no due date and no one will see it but you – so you can be honest. Your assignment will be to rank and write out the priorities in your heart and then rank and write out the priorities that currently dominate your life. Then you will compare how the life rankings measure up to your heart rankings. Hint: your life should line up with your heart's desires. The book concludes with a call for you to chase real rabbits a lot more often and inspire others to do the same.

I KNOW WHAT YOU'RE THINKING: THERE ARE MOUNTAINS OF BOOKS ON HAPPINESS

You may wonder, "Isn't this just another of the thousand books out there that tell me how to be happy?" Well, yes and no. Yes, this is a book that lays out a plan for you to be happy. That is absolutely my goal and I hope you pay attention. But, this is not the typical self-help book that offers some quick fixes (clean the house, go shopping) or platitudes (affirm your greatness in the mirror twice daily). I will not require you to meditate in the mountains for a month and ponder your life or buy a motorcycle. There are no stories of big-time executives who found the key to happiness in the wee hours at the office (this is very, very uncommon) or calls to quit your job tomorrow (though your priorities homework might encourage an eventual career change).

My approach is significantly different. This book uses character and integrity as the vehicles to develop a real and lasting happiness. It digs deep – this is a serious subject with a ton at stake. It is also fast-paced, fun, and humorous. I take this tack because we are all human and our search for happiness can be a comedy of errors at times. Mine sure has been as you will see in CHAPTER 1. The idea is for you to stay engaged by thinking deeply, reflecting, and smiling as we embark on this journey together.

Most importantly, though, this book is different because it advocates for a balanced approach to finding happiness. You need not move into a bare-bones abode, wear raggedly old clothes, avoid makeup, shun wealth, or ignore whether people like and look up to you. None of these sacrifices are necessary for you to achieve authentic happiness. Instead, I will tell you time and again that those worldly things do indeed matter but not nearly as much as you think. They are not nearly as important as waking up happy, finding a few good friends, and developing your character. Follow this recipe and increase your chances of finding authentic happiness. Then, you'll be glad you picked up <u>this</u> book on happiness from the colossal stack.

I KNOW WHAT YOU'RE THINKING: WHO ARE YOU TO JUDGE ME?

One final note. I am keenly aware that people bristle whenever <u>their</u> character development is on the table. It's okay to talk about the subject in the abstract or pick on other people. But, personalize and critically evaluate someone's ethical struggles and watch out! Moral relativism and anger take over and people exclaim, "Don't judge me! This is my life and I'll figure it out! Who are you to tell me how to live? You're no better than I am!" I've even had one person write to me after a speech, "You're not God, you can't judge me!" Those reactions are powerful and designed to push people away. It's tough to want to help someone who responds like that. However, I have studied and spoken about ethics and character long enough to understand and appreciate these reactions. Being criticized on how I lived my life used to grate on me too – especially when someone close to me was the antagonist. Older and wiser now, I wish I would have listened more attentively to my friends and loved ones.

So, I am acutely aware that some of the following thoughts (or even whole chapters) might make you mad. But, I ask you to fight that reaction and work through it. Please understand the sincere spirit from which my advice comes. I earnestly want you to be authentically happy too. I want to live in a world where more people experience this feeling. Such a world will make my encounters with you in the airport more pleasant. It will make your family life stronger and your work life more satisfying for you and your colleagues (happy employees build morale). It will make average business transactions more pleasant and honest. Maybe it will even improve our political culture (I can dream).

But, most importantly, I have two daughters! They are precious little humans and it is my nightly prayer that they grow up in a world where more people are content and kind, where relationships are stronger and more authentic, and where people are good to each other solely because it is the right thing to do. I want you to be a leader in a world that encourages them to discover their authentic happiness. So, let us take this journey together. Keep an open mind and let us see if I can convince you to buy in. Enjoy the ride!

PART I:

ON YOUR MARK

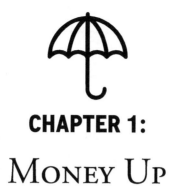

CHAPTER 1:

MONEY UP

"Don't get so busy making a living that you forget to make a life."
– Dolly Parton

"You can love your job ... but your job will not love you back."
– Cathie Black

Settle in for a remarkable story. It depicts a decade of following conventional wisdom. It is a tale at the intersection of worldly success, confused priorities, and educated cluelessness. It features a young person who bought into the hype – the idea that wealth, good looks, and the esteem of others can make a person authentically happy. Sound familiar? That describes most everyone at some point, I suppose.

Let me be more specific. This is a story about someone trying to "money up" to success.[2] In other words, a decent person employing education, brains, and plenty of time hoping to get rich, get fancy stuff, and finally get recognized as successful. All this was done to meet the presumed prerequisites to happiness. Our protagonist operated with an astute plan and plenty of drive but without authentic success as the goal. To be sure, there were many positives along the way – a great education, interesting acquaintances, success under pressure, and sophisticated work. But, in the end, these tremendous efforts constituted nothing more than an abstract failure to chase real rabbits and discover real happiness. Far into the ascent, it became clear that this ladder to "success" was indeed leaning against the wrong wall.[3]

Pathetically … the story is my own. I learned a great deal from these events; they certainly shaped my character and purpose in life. I am blessed by my travails. My story transformed me from lawyer to teacher, inspired this book, and solidified a platform to influence hundreds of thousands of people with this message. Nevertheless, the whole thing beat me up mentally and physically and left me exhausted. I hope my lessons prove enlightening and save you similar agony.

Your homework is to use my story to ponder your life – particularly the things you chase. Are they real or fake? Are you happy or not so much? As you read along, picture what you chased (or continue to chase) at each stage of your life. Chances are you will be surprised by the similarities of our journeys. Perhaps you will be inspired to make some key changes and begin to chase what really matters in life.

---

2   This reminds me of the saying "cowboy up" – i.e., to round up desire and determination to overcome a formidable challenge. To cowboy up means to try extraordinarily hard to achieve a difficult goal. To me, to "money up" is a corollary. It's basically the trying extraordinarily hard to put yourself in a place where you become wealthy and professionally successful. From there, you use that success as a springboard to happiness. This is not about playing the lottery or other quick fixes. This is a serious strategy employed by serious people. They often fail to seek happiness via the chase of real rabbits because their pursuit of wealth and prestige takes up all their time and bandwidth. And, that's what makes the attempt to money up so dangerous.

3   Joseph Campbell said, "There is perhaps nothing worse than reaching the top of the ladder and discovering that you're on the wrong wall."

COLLEGE, LAW SCHOOL & THE LITTLE VOICE IN MY HEAD

I am a first-generation college student. My parents never finished college but jumped at the chance for me to have the experience and education. Their message was, "We're not quite sure what to tell you … so just go and please don't screw it up." Clueless, I arrived on campus excited to study American History or Political Science. These topics made me curious. But, I had this little aggravating yet persuasive voice in the back of my head. It wouldn't stop chattering. Every time I made a serious decision (such as choosing a major or picking a summer job) and followed my heart, the little voice reiterated its primary argument: "Corey, you get an education to move up in life – both in income and class. Corey, you go to college to land a fancy job and earn respect so that you become rich and successful. This is why everyone is here. This is why college is so expensive. This is why there are only 30 History majors and 2,500 business majors on campus." And on and on it went. This voice has likely reared its ugly head in your life at some point. Perhaps it still speaks to you. I now have mine on mute!

My little voice was compelling. The advice it doled out was legitimized as I saw other people chasing similar goals. This mass of people knew what they were doing, right? I quickly realized that I'd never become rich as a History major – an accurate assessment perhaps but an unfortunate miscalculation. So, I changed my major to Business. I didn't love studying the intricacies of business like accounting statements and management theory. However, I thought I had located an on-ramp to the road to prosperity. Shortly thereafter, several of my friends applied to law school and I thought, "Corey, that's the ticket! If you become a lawyer, you can have all this times ten. All your friends with their fancy business degrees will seek your legal counsel. You will earn a big office and the respect of your community." I didn't exactly want to be a lawyer. But, again, I thought that this was the means to a big house, a fancy car, a prestigious job and, ultimately, happiness. I had taken one INTRODUCTION TO LAW class as an undergraduate, studied hard for the LSAT, scored high enough, and was accepted to Duke Law School. Surely that was enough to choose a three-year legal education and a legal career.

Fast forward several years ... I graduated and now faced my first serious real-world, professional dilemma. Ask yourself what you would do under these circumstances:

- You just graduated from a great law school where nearly everyone takes a job in law;
- You accumulated over $120,000 in student loans to become a lawyer;
- You, therefore, need a job to buy things, pay bills, and service this debt;
- You are not drawn to the practice of law; but
- You still have those fancy cars and a big house on the agenda

So, what would you do? You would become a lawyer, of course. I was as novice a lawyer as you could find, but at least I had some legal knowledge. Other than that, I had experience teaching tennis as a summer job throughout school. But, that type of career was not what I would call a "Plan B" – not with my goals. And ... the little voice was still there and now it was amplified. "Corey, you went to law school so that you could become rich. Now is your chance. Look at the high paying jobs your classmates are getting. Get out there and get hired at the best firm you can. Get your high salary and five figure year-end bonus. Let's do this." In my mind, there were only two options: (1) go be a lawyer or (2) bust.

TO BE OR NOT TO BE ... A LAWYER

I chose to become a lawyer. It sounded better than "bust." This decision kicked off my "I want to be a corporate lawyer" interview process. I went to a prestigious law school; this fact alone afforded its graduates many advantages. A lot of firms were interested in me based solely on my pedigree. These jobs paid a lot of money and came with the many perks I imagined in the form of chances to travel the world, floor seats at basketball games, offices high up in sky scrapers – "rarefied air" as my classmates called it. The little voice's plan was working to perfection.

I passed through many law firms during these interviews. Some were family-friendly and the people seemed happy. They worked normal hours and got weekends off (like most sane people). Other places seemed like high-paying sweatshops where lawyers labored around the clock. Sounds like an easy choice, right? Just choose the firm with the highest morale, right? Wrong! The family friendly, happy firms just didn't pay enough for my ego. My law school friends were making much more money at more prestigious places. I decided to keep moving up the chain to interview at more elite establishments. I used my job offers at the happy places to parlay my way into interviews at the rarefied-air firms. I knew they paid more. The little voice was happy.

During each interview, a lawyer would ask me if I had any questions. The Career Services office had trained us thoroughly for these moments. This was my chance to ask: (1) what kind of clients they represented, (2) how the partnership track worked, and (3) whether we got to rotate through practice areas. What I wanted to know the most, however, was how much they paid. So, I would always ask this question at the end of my interview.

Keep in mind that teenagers applying to be summer lifeguards know enough not to ask questions about money during an interview. Pay talk should always come after the offer of employment. But, I was laser focused on this issue and this issue alone. The interviewers would look awkwardly at each other and then at me, humor me, and uncomfortably respond with a salary range.

THE LAW FIRM BATHROOM

At one firm, I interviewed with a partner who seemed to like me. In answer to my salary inquiry, she explained, "We pay $120,000 a year to our new associates – that's $10,000 a month. It's the most you'll make in Denver as a young lawyer."

Those were the magic words. I beamed inside. I reacted quickly and without really thinking, "I'm in! I'll take it."

She looked back at me, chuckled and said, "Calm down. This is just an interview. We need to like you too. We'll send you home after lunch and then evaluate you and everyone else we're interviewing later this week. If the stars align, we will give you an offer. It's really competitive to get a job here … so no promises."

It was obvious that I was a little too nervous for my own good. She could tell and said, "I can tell you're nervous. Do you need to use the bathroom before your next interview, take a little break? The bathroom is out my door, down the hall, and to the right." What she implied was, "You're asking weird questions. You seem preoccupied with the salary and don't seem focused enough on what we do around here. I like you and want my colleagues to like you too. So, go to the bathroom and reset." This was sort of like what parents do to their kids when they send them to their room for a timeout. And, let's keep in mind that I was just asked at the age of 25 if I needed to go to the bathroom!

"Yes. Please." I said, relieved to leave and start fresh in the next lawyer's office. Off I went … down the hall and to the right.

Standing in front of the bathroom door was a young associate. You can easily separate the young associates at prestigious law firms like this because most fit a pattern: they wear expensive suits, nervously fidget, rarely smile and generally appear uncomfortable and exhausted. It's like they want to scream for help all day but don't want to waste the billable hours. I saw him there and he saw me. As I approached the door, he pointed and said, "You!" and followed me into the bathroom.

Have you ever had someone you don't know stalk you into a bathroom? Probably not. Have you ever had that happen to you at a job interview? Trust me … it's awkward. I sensed him on my heels so I went to the sink and washed my hands. It got worse. He walked up and slowly put his arm around me. Have you ever had someone you don't know put his arm around you … in a bathroom … at a job interview? Awkward doesn't do this experience justice – especially in a men's restroom where you can hear a pin drop 99% of the time. It got even worse. He leaned in and started to whisper in my ear. I looked in the mirror and thought, "What in the world is happening? I'm either going to get asked out or beat up. Please God, let this end."

But things were moving too quickly. He never smiled and creepily whispered, "Your name is Corey, right?"

Understanding that he had more information that I did and figuring it was best that we both whisper, I told the truth, "Uhh, yeah."

He whispered, "You went to Duke Law School, right?"

"Uhh, yeah."

"Well I went there too. We're supposed to stick together, us alumni. So, I'm going to give you the best piece of professional advice you will ever received." He leaned closer and said, "Don't come work here. You'll hate this place and they will grow to hate you. Many of these people are exceptionally mean to each other and they aren't happy. A lot of them never see their families. You'll work so hard that you'll keep a suitcase behind the door. That way you can change clothes when you spend the night here. They'll pay you a lot of money but they'll work you to the bone for it. Trust me. You should fake an illness and leave now."

Then … he hustled out the door. I didn't see that guy the rest of my interview day. For obvious reasons, he was not included on the official interview team. He disappeared and I just stood in front of the mirror in shock.

What I realize now is that a normal person in that moment would think, "Well … that's a red flag. I probably shouldn't work here. That conversation was not in that guy's best interest. He could be fired for speaking that way to me – I was a potential employee. Therefore, he must be telling the truth. I think I'll take this firm off my list."

As you might imagine, that conversation never took place in my head. Instead, I rationalized his advice away. "That guy is crazy. He's wrong. This place has so much appeal on paper. He is probably just a lone, jaded wolf. Every company has a few." Plus, I had already bought a BMW. Those are expensive. I was ready to put an earnest money deposit down on a house. The builder required certified funds. I craved nice clothes. It was time to travel the world. I wanted all the perks that a job like this provided. So, I counted his opinion as an outlier and went on with my interview. I pulled it together the rest of the day and asked better questions. I was fortunate enough to receive an offer a few weeks later.

MY FIRST & LAST LAW FIRM JOB

My first day at work was upon me. Even though I was a brand new and clueless young attorney, it didn't take long to figure out that my acquaintance from the bathroom was right. By the end of my first day on the job, I had already messed something up. It was a small snafu, but it was a mistake in a document that a partner had to spend time to fix. He burst into my office and slammed my door so hard that a picture fell off the wall. No pleasantries to start this meeting. I knew his name and admired his successful corporate law practice, but I bet he knew nothing about me. The drubbing went like this:

PARTNER (throwing a manila folder marked "Confidential" on the floor with its contents spilling throughout my office): "Are you an idiot or something?"

ME: Caught off-guard, deer in the headlights. No response.

PARTNER: "We're not paying you this much money to make these mistakes. What the hell were you thinking? I don't have time to do this first-year law school stuff for my associates."

ME: Deer in the headlights, still silent but now at least thinking: "This is my first day! What did I do wrong? Can you please be a bit more specific so I can make it right? Maybe I am an idiot or something."

PARTNER: "Never again or you're out of here! Do you hear me? There are hundreds of young lawyers just like you, just as qualified as you, who would love to work here. Never again!" He reopened the door, stormed out, and slammed it for the second time. Thankfully, there was nothing left on my wall to crash to the ground.

"Ok." I thought, "Well, that sucked. I'm still not sure what I did wrong. But, I can deal with one jerk in possession of terrible people skills. Did he want his folder back?"

I spent my first evening as an employed lawyer (until around midnight) scanning through the papers on my floor trying to figure out what I did wrong. All for $300 per hour that I clearly wasn't worth. Had he just pointed out my mistake, I could have fixed it. I'd be done and home by now. But this was trial by fire. The time-tested mantra at places like this is: "You screwed up … now you figure it out and fix it. That's the way we've always taught young attorneys." That partner never asked to work with me and rarely spoke to me again. Once you mess up, they find another young associate to test drive.

The Beginning of the End

Things deteriorated from there. It's safe and rather sad to say that Day One for me was the beginning of the end of my legal career. The daily grind was much worse than my Day One experience. It soon became my largest stressor and began to affect my personality and relationships. There just wasn't time to take a mental break or hang out with friends. I had all this money but there was no time to spend it. I'd come in at 8:00 am and everything was closed. I'd leave around 10:00 pm and everything was closed. I would sneak to the gym at lunch using the side stairs to get to a lower floor and then duck and dodge to another set of stairs to get to another floor where I felt safe to wait for the elevator. People who saw me asked me why I was leaving the office for lunch. Their lunch was delivered and on their desk.

About six months into the job, we were corporate counsel on a huge deal. It was an initial public offering worth around $200 million. That type of deal generates large lawyer fees and immense pressure. Everyone wanted to do it right and avoid bad press. There is much that can go wrong in these types of deals. We were bound to silence so as not to influence the market or be charged with insider trading. I didn't dare even tell my fiancé what I was doing at work for hours and hours at a time. The little details in deals like this really matter. Therefore, it was all hands on deck. I barely went home for an entire week. A continuous dose of that pressure and lack of sleep will take years off your life. I did indeed have a suitcase behind my door full of suits and toiletries. They rented us hotel rooms across the street. These rooms were not to sleep in, mind you, but just to shower and change so we didn't stink for upcoming client meetings.

Even if we weren't busy all the time during the deal, we were expected to be there – waiting and anticipating the next document to come back from the printer or the Securities and Exchange Commission. We would watch the news in China. Why? If something exploded in China, then the Dow Jones average would likely go down the next day in America and our IPO might be called off. Executives desperately want their IPOs to close in an up-trending market. I tried to get a little sleep in my chair. Proving fruitless, I would wander the halls and head over the partner side of the office. This is where the bosses' offices were and I was snooping to see if there was any activity this late.

I thought, "It's Monday morning at 3:00 am. Surely the bosses are home in bed. The plebs like me are the only ones here, just in case."

But they weren't. They were there – emailing, yelling at someone, talking on the phone. They were hard at work.

Figuring this an aberration, I walked back around to that part of the office several more times that week in the early morning hours. These people were still there, still working. They were emailing, yelling at someone, talking on the phone. I observed this for a full week and the truth finally hit me:

That guy from the bathroom was right. This job does suck. These people are always here. They have families. They have kids and spouses at home who they never see. They seem consistently unhappy and treat each other poorly. They look like they want to cry on a daily basis.

I need to quit!

This is not a conversation you want to have with yourself. This is especially true after you've put in nearly a decade and spent hundreds of thousands of dollars to get to this point. What do you do in situations like this? Well, you call someone who loves you. So, I called my fiancé (now wife). She answered a bit groggy and I said, "Honey I hate this job. I'm here late … again. Everyone is miserable. I'm miserable. I can't tell you when I'll be home next. I've decided that I really need to quit. You're okay with that, right?"

My wife is an awesome person, as good as it gets. She is patient and kind. And, she's generally super supportive. Generally, she will say things like, "Ok. We've been through hard times before and we can get through this. I'll stick with you and we'll put our heads together and figure it out." But not this morning. I must have shocked her with my comments. Or, she had a different plan for how my law career would end. Who knows? Regardless, she replied, "Corey, I never intended on marrying a quitter."

"Uhhh, excuse me? Wait, what?" I said. That backfired. She wasn't supposed to say that. And, if I'd known she was going to say that, I would have called my mom instead! My mom would have been a lot more supportive. My mom would have said something like, "Honey, just go do what makes you happy. Go pay back your law school loans by mowing lawns or teaching tennis again." However, I didn't have my mom on the phone; it was still my fiancé who then said, "Corey, what else do you know how to do? Do you have any other skills? You can't just quit."

She was killing me at this point. But I knew she was right. Like I said, I knew how to teach tennis well and I kind of knew how to be a lawyer. Her point was that I had trained all these years for this job and I had barely given it a chance. I just didn't have much else to offer the world yet. We agreed that staying was the least risky option for my career, my reputation, and my pocketbook. I promised her I wouldn't quit for at least six more months.

I Quit (Six Months Later of course)

On the six-month anniversary of the phone call with my wife, I drove in to work with my letter of resignation. I remember putting a lot of heart into this document. This firm had been good enough to give me a job in the post dot-com economy where there was a dearth of corporate lawyer jobs, pay me a lot of money, and teach me (in their own special way) how to be a lawyer. I was grateful.

I took my letter down to my senior partner's office. My hands were shaking. This was as scared as I'd ever been in a professional setting. I knocked on his door and asked to come in. I chose this partner because we were friendly. He tended to have the back of the junior associates. I handed him the letter and told him that I was resigning. I offered to stay for two weeks or however long they needed me. I'll never forget what happened next.

"Shut up, Corey. Nobody quits." He took my letter, ripped it in half and threw it in his trash can by my feet. Well, neither business school nor law school taught me what to do when the boss rips up your resignation letter and throws it in the trash can. I was scanning the office, looking around like the patsy in a John Grisham novel. I thought to myself, "I can leave, right? There's not someone behind me with a gun to my head? What do you mean I can't quit?" It was surreal.

For some reason his actions emboldened me. I snapped, "What do you mean no one quits? In my opinion, nearly everyone who works here is completely and utterly miserable."

He responded with such a flat affect that I knew he was dead serious, "That's true. They are miserable."

So, I tried a different tack. "Well, there a ton of people here on their third to fifth marriages. This job is at least partially responsible for ruining those relationships."

"That's true too," he responded curtly.

He saw me floundering and finally decided to bail me out. "You're right. This is a very difficult job. There's a ton of money at stake and these big corporate transactions facilitate economic growth. We make sure these Fortune 500 businesses meet complicated legal obligations detailed in thousands of constantly changing regulations. When you have a job that hard which requires so many hours for so many years to be done right, a lot of people are going to be miserable. It's just the tradeoff. Their personal relationships struggle and they aren't happy because all they do is work. But they don't quit. And there are generally two reasons why."

"That doesn't make any sense. Please tell me why," I asked inquisitively.

"First, a lot of them are broke. Just flat broke."

"Broke!" I exclaimed. "A lot of these people make $500,000 a year or more. And they've made this kind of cash for decades. How can they be broke?"

He responded with a very simple truth that describes many Americans today: "Corey, it doesn't matter how much we pay these people, they always spend more than they have. They spend their salary and then, when that runs out, they accumulate credit card debt. They should have bought a million-dollar house but they bought a three-million-dollar house. Do you know what the mortgage payment is on a three-million-dollar house? It's over $17,000 a month! They should drive BMW 3 Series but they all have BMW 650s and 700s. They should fly coach with their kids to Europe, but they always fly the family first class. It gets damn expensive."

"In the end, they are paid handsomely but they always want more. So, they are broke. They desperately need this job to fund their lifestyles and ambitions."

He was reiterating a fundamental truth that any eighth grader could tell you: if you spend more money than you have, you will go broke. I knew, of course, that this applied to the average person; I knew that people making $50,000 would be broke if they spent $60,000 a year. I just thought that people making over half a million dollars a year would be ok. I was wrong.

I asked, "What's the second reason they stay?"

"Well, that's almost worse than the first," said the partner. "The second reason no one quits is pride. Lawyers are a prideful bunch. What are they going to do, Corey, quit being lawyers and go wait tables at Chili's?"

This one caught me off guard as well. It seemed obvious that there had to be a middle ground between being a big time corporate lawyer and waiting tables! The more I thought about it though, the more I got it. You don't just go from being a corporate lawyer to being a judge. That's rare and difficult. You don't switch from being a corporate lawyer to hanging your shingle in private practice. In the same way, you don't just go become a prosecutor. If you're a pediatrician, you don't just go become a surgeon because you don't like sick kids anymore. You must go back and complete a different educational program. It's incredibly hard to start over once you're ensconced in a career. This is particularly tough on a successful person's pride.

He continued, "It's the pride that gets them. They are scared to go home at Thanksgiving and tell their families and friends that they quit their job at this prestigious law firm. They want to say they are doing better than their siblings and their peers from high school, college, and grad school. So, they stay."

I could tell this conversation was almost over. I'd just wasted thirty minutes of this man's time ($250 based on his $500 hourly billing rate) on questions he found so simple. In the end, he thought I should have known the deal before signing up to take the piles of cash. I was told all this, of course – in the bathroom during my interview – but that advice fell on deaf ears. But, I had heard today's conversation loud and clear.

I looked at my letter of resignation in the trash, looked at him, and walked out of his office. I conspicuously took the main elevator this time and went to play basketball at lunch. What were they going to do, disregard my resignation and fire me? It didn't matter. There was no way I was using these people as professional references. Two weeks later my career as a corporate lawyer was officially over – just over one year after I started. The relief I felt that day was like nothing I had ever experienced. I had been bold to quit and brimming with the desire to be authentically happy. I didn't have a job lined up or any plans really. But, I was now free to live a different life, to structure my priorities the way my heart desired. I could go to sleep whenever and wherever I wanted, proudly walk to the gym at noon to play basketball and eat lunch on a real table, not a desk cluttered with papers. I could breathe again.

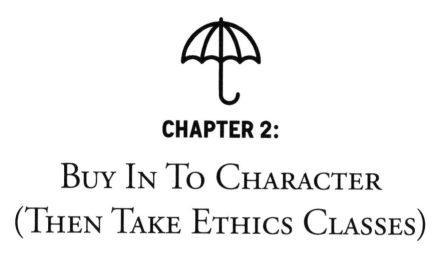

CHAPTER 2:

BUY IN TO CHARACTER (THEN TAKE ETHICS CLASSES)

"Good character is not formed in a week or a month. It is created little by little, day by day. Protracted and patient effort is needed to develop good character."
— Heraclitus (Greek philosopher)

"I have an unending desire to be better and make myself a better person."
— Tanya Tucker

As I celebrated six months of freedom from law firm captivity, my phone rang. The caller ID read, "UNIVERSITY OF DENVER." On the line was a professor from the Business Ethics and Legal Studies Department. He informed me that his colleague had just passed away. This professor had been a legend on campus and very professionally accomplished. It was a sad time but the school needed to fill this position ASAP – students had registered for the fall term. I landed on his radar after inquiring about adjuncting a class. Adjuncts teach one class every two years or so, just for fun. I was looking for a compelling way keep my legal training sharp. But now, this man was asking me if I would apply to be a full-time professor.

I had never felt the desire to be a teacher. Lecturing, researching, and publishing journal articles for a living was not a focus. I admired my professors, but my future was more entrepreneurial. I just opened a small business which ran tennis and basketball camps for kids. Remember, according to my wife, that's the only other job skill I possessed. I hired 20 employees and I was the boss. I relished my freedom and worked outside in the Colorado sun. I helped kids gain confidence through sports and that made me happy. I played basketball at lunch and worked from home with ESPN on in the background. There were early mornings and late nights to be sure, but my days revolved around a schedule which I created and approved. My life was my own again. This was my future. Therefore, I demurred.

The professor asked me to at least come down for an interview. He employed the strategy my wife and I use to encourage our three-year-old to eat, "Try it. You just might like it." These are the types of favors you do for your alma mater. So, I reluctantly agreed.

I returned to the DU campus for the first time in years. It was a crisp, late summer day. Students were bustling to and fro. People seemed friendly and the campus was beautiful. It brought back memories of college – where I should have studied American History! I gave a mock lecture and sat for one-on-one interviews with department members. During a memorable interview a professor inquired, "I have some tough questions for you. We get that you know how to teach law. You have an interesting legal background."

I chuckled sheepishly at his use of the phrase, "interesting legal background."

"We get that you know something about business; you run an intriguing small business. But what about ethics? You will have to teach ethics classes too. This is the Law and Ethics Department in our business school. So … what do you know about ethics?"

Before I could respond, he peppered me with the following questions: "Can you define character for me? Are you a person of high moral character and why? Do you have a favorite ethical decision-making approach? Why does it matter to you to be a moral actor?"

These were fair and yet genuinely perplexing questions. They came rapid fire and stumped me. How would you have answered them on the spot? What does it mean to you to be a person of high moral character? What ethical decision-making approach do you utilize daily to grind through ethical grey areas? Are you a moral actor and, if so, why and how often? I had no good answers so I told the awkward truth.

I said, "I really don't know much about ethics [long pause]. I went to law school, remember? We were busy studying other things. Ask me about the Securities and Exchange Commission rules and regulations, please."

I was not trying to be cute. I just did not see my legal curriculum as an ethics education. I could not speak intelligently about ethical issues at the intersection of law and business. That topic never came up. And I certainly could not speak to the recipe for living an ethical life. I had put very little thought into these noble issues. I was busy living my life. I was certainly not thinking about how my morality or lack thereof continually affected myself and society.

I felt ashamed. I supposed everyone should be thinking about these important issues if we desire our community, nation, and world to be a better, more moral place. This was his point. I reached for an answer. Like most people, my ethical decisions came straight from my gut. I did what I felt was right. Doing the right thing mattered to me but only in the abstract. I did not have any specific ethical decision-making framework to fall back on when my gut failed me. I did not analyze my duties as a member of a community or whether my decisions would produce the greatest good for the greatest number of people. I had never evaluated whether my actions habitually aligned with my virtues. But, I did think that I was a pretty good person. Doesn't most everyone? Going with my gut had led to some pretty poor ethical decisions in my past, that's true. But, it also produced many outcomes of which I was proud. I certainly was not going to bring any of this up. Not now.

He pushed, "But you took an ethics class in law school, right? Everyone must take that class to graduate. It's required. So, you must know something about ethics. Tell me you've thought about this stuff. Did you pass that class?"

"That's true," I replied. "I did have to take that class. We all did. And I passed … with a B, I think. To me, though, that curriculum wasn't really about ethics at all – at least in the character and moral development sense that interests you. It certainly did not make me a better person."

SEGUE: THE REQUIRED LEGAL ETHICS CLASS

Let me pause and depict the required legal ethics class. Picture a classroom full of overachieving graduate students – each eager to earn one of the few A grades on the table. Everyone piles into a classroom and the tension is palpable. Every day in law school is like that. Every class creates a fear of getting called on, messing up, and publicly confirming how little you know. You prepare not so much to learn but to avoid looking foolish in front of your peers. Eventually every student falls prey to the inevitable and says something silly, or idiotic, or worse.[4] A distinguished law professor arrives precisely on time, slams a thick (think 1,200 page) casebook on the podium, and says something to the effect of:

"This is Legal Ethics. The most important class you take in law school. The legal field needs more ethical professionals. Lawyers in the country have a bad name. Classes like these help remediate that perception. Plus, you don't want to

---

4   Here's a funny side note on law students saying something foolish, idiotic, or worse: I was once asked to read a paragraph directly from a book by an intimidating Contracts professor. He was already steaming because the first student he asked to read was apparently hungover and replied, "I'm just happy to be here today, sir." The second student he asked tried to be funny and said, "Read? No, I'll take the physical challenge instead." The professor scowled as everyone else sat in horror. I was third in the row and next. It was no big deal, just read words from a book out loud in front of the class. But, I was so scared of being called on and the ensuing follow up questions that I couldn't even read. I was paralyzed. The professor said, in his thick German accent, "Corey, you must read from the page. Just read from the page. You cannot even do this? Who can help Corey read from the page? Lawyers must be able to read, Corey." And then he moved to the person next to me, a wunderkind who could actually read! On that day, only one of four law students could read words (in English), out loud from a book. This wasn't the first time I looked like a fool in front of my law school classmates, but it's the one I remember most embarrassingly. I hope this tale helps you evaluate the palpably tense Legal Ethics classroom environment as well.

be disbarred for unethical behavior, do you? Therefore, you will all be reading this book."

Everyone shudders. Many squirm. A few do the math: 1,200 pages of legal ethics (pages filled with legalese that will require a re-read) plus similar reading for my other four classes. That's around 300 pages of dense law reading a week … for seventeen weeks. Yikes!

The ethics professor continues, "This book contains ethical rules for lawyers. We call these the Rules of Professional Conduct. You will read these rules many times and evaluate legal decisions penalizing lawyers who go rogue. So please read this book, think deeply about these rules, memorize some of them, and you will find yourself on the path of an ethical attorney. Plus, there is a special examination on ethics – it's called the Multistate Professional Responsibility Exam. You must pass to be a member of the legal bar in all but a handful of states. You do not want to fail that test. Law firms despise law school graduates who fail the ethics test. These firms have core values revolving around ethics and hires perceived as unethical are bad for the brand." The professor inevitably then mentions that lawyers must complete continuing ethics education courses each year and that people tend bristle at the added burden to their already busy lives. And off you go for a semester's worth of required ethics training.

In my class, the conversations were interesting and the bevy of violations shocking. We observed that plenty of lawyers fail to abide by these simple rules – some flounder on multiple occasions. Perhaps unsurprisingly, this blatantly unethical behavior is often part of a conspiracy with businesspeople, government officials, and/or other professionals. These case studies were designed to demonstrate the consequences suffered by cheaters and, thereby, encourage ethical behavior. The thesis of this class boiled down to: <u>Follow these minimum standards and you will avoid punishment, remain in good professional standing, and be viewed as an ethical attorney</u>. There was nothing about honing the virtuous character traits of an ethical attorney or leaving the profession better than we found it. Little was said about maximizing the well-being of others besides the general restriction against screwing people over. There were few, if any, conversations about whether we would want to live in a world where lawyers acted unethically and what that meant about how we should act. Staying true to our consciences rarely came up.

This approach began to perplex me. I kept thinking, "It can't be this easy, right? Just read a book, enroll in a class, take a two-hour test, follow the rules, and ... poof ... become an ethical attorney. There must be something more, something in a person's heart driving them to act morally, right? The disincentive of being disbarred looms large I suppose, but is it powerful enough to create long-lasting and sincere ethical behavior? Is the shame of losing a law license the best way to create morality? And, if every lawyer in America is required to pass this class in law school, why are there still casebooks full of recent violations of legal ethics? How come the reputation of lawyers nationwide still stinks?"[5] Why aren't there fewer and fewer ethical violations by lawyers? This somber inquisition still makes my head hurt.

Ethics Inculcation v. Buy In

The powers-that-be seek to motivate ethical behavior via inculcation as opposed to buy in. The two concepts are similar with a subtle, very important, difference. To inculcate means: "to instill by forceful or insistent repetition; to implant by repeated statement or admonition or to influence someone to accept an idea or feeling."[6] Inculcation can certainly influence behavior and disseminate ideas but acceptance is rarely authentic or deeply-held.

For example, it's considered poor form when a professor influences students to adopt certain political views. Students quickly realize that they need to say the right thing or risk being embarrassed in lecture and graded poorly. A teacher

---

5   An Australian magazine looked to popular opinion (i.e., Facebook) to find out why so many people hate lawyers. The answers came back predictably: "Three main causes for the bad reputation of lawyers emerged from the [responses]: (1) lawyers 'cost shiploads' and 'come across as leeches feeding off human suffering'; (2) ignorance of the law and legal ethics generates unfair stereotypes; and (3) lawyers are 'smart arses' with 'egos the size of Texas.'" *Why Do People Hate Lawyers So Much?* LAWYER'S WEEKLY, February 18, 2015, http://tiny.cc/edkshy. The American public has similar feelings. *See The Four Reasons We Hate Lawyers,* LEGAL SHIELD.COM, June 22, 2015, http://tinyurl.com/h2asnwn.
6   See The Free Dictionary.com and Dictionary.com, http://www.thefreedictionary.com/inculcateDictionary.com and http://www.dictionary.com/browse/inculcate.

sits in a positon of power, controls grades, writes recommendation letters, and speaks from a bully pulpit. After such inculcation, students tend to echo a teacher's ideology in class (for all the wrong reasons) but rarely become true believers. Classroom inculcation is all too common, unfortunately. The good news is that these newfound beliefs are unlikely to take root because they are formed improperly. Such students are just as likely to mimic their next professor's ideological bent or the current cause célèbre on social media.

Buy in, on the other hand, occurs when a person ponders an idea, weighs the pros and cons, and accepts it as meaningful on its own merits. This approach is remarkable because acceptance occurs without the use of force or coercion. Nothing need be instilled by repeated admonition or undue influence. In fact, coercion is frowned upon when it comes to obtaining true buy in. This is a purer, more authentic, form of idea acceptance. Beliefs formed via buy in tend to stick.

When it comes to ethics, the legal community forces inculcation when it should seek buy in. The strategy is to motivate ethical behavior by repeated, mandatory contact with the topic. This regimen is supposed to influence lawyers to accept the idea that legal ethics matter and that it is crucial to follow the rules. These requirements also assure the public that the profession is trying to regulate itself in ethically appropriate ways. This goal is legitimate. The "lawyer-as-moral-actor" brand could surely be stronger. More importantly, ethical lawyers help ensure that the American justice system retains its credibility as the model for the world. The problem is that the map directing lawyers to these admirable goals is missing a crucial quadrant.

True character development requires buy in, as early in the process as possible, rather than inculcation. A person sitting unwillingly through the mandatory inculcation process will resemble a student who parrots back ideological views to get a good grade. Enough will be done to pass the course but the information will fly in one ear and out the other. A person who buys in to the idea that character matters, on the other hand, is more likely to see the curriculum as important and reap the most benefits from ethics instruction. Only with buy in will ethics classes have the desired effect.

Before you judge legal education too harshly, realize that many other professions also employ similar ethics inculcation tactics. Take accounting, architecture, engineering, financial planning, graphic arts, medicine, real estate, and social work, for example.[7] These highly educated professionals are also required to ponder ethics on occasion or suffer the consequences. They may take a few ethics classes, find themselves governed by rules of professional conduct, glide through a bit of mandatory continuing ethics education, and think about ethical dilemmas for the required forty or so hours a year. Many professionals do not desire to do all this, of course. It is time consuming and expensive. But they either get these credits or face losing their license and becoming professionally ostracized.

So, Are Professional Standards Worthwhile?

I believe that most professionals are upstanding, ethical people and I have no problem with mandatory ethics classes or codes. Professionals are responsible for our most precious assets (our lives, our health, our souls, our freedom, our retirements, etc.). This means that they toil under extremely difficult conditions and constantly confront ethical gray areas. Professional boundaries must be set and enforced.

Therefore, professional organizations should be commended for having rules of ethical conduct and encouraging and training professionals to comply. My problem rests in the idea that this is all a person must do to cover the bases and be considered an ethical professional. The process all but ignores the fact that buying in to being a good person is significant. Without any encouragement to engage in character-based thinking and development, as opposed to merely covering tedious and abstract rules, many professionals will pass the ethics classes and still slip through the cracks.

If you disagree, please ponder this very serious question:

---

7   There is even a Center for the Study of Ethics in the Professions run out of the Illinois Institute of Technology. This group collects and categorizes the codes of ethics or rules of professional conduct for dozens and dozens of professions. See http://ethics.iit.edu/ecodes/.

If every lawyer, doctor, Certified Public Accountant, Certified Financial Analyst, etc. in America is required to take professional ethics classes, read, think deeply about, and be tested on these professional standards ... how come so many lawyers, doctors, accountants, and financial professionals, etc. still cross ethical boundaries? Why do so many cheat, defraud, and mislead the public? Why doesn't the public revere these professionals as ethical exemplars? How are these fraudsters allowed through the ethical checkpoints?

THE PROOF IS IN THE PUDDING

You know as well as I do that, even after all the resources plowed into ethics education and training, cheating remains rampant. It occurs in business, academia, sports, journalism, politics, and anywhere else competition is king. Many fiascos become front page news[8] while others cause harm more covertly. [9] Most of us still recoil when the names of companies involved old ethics scandals come up in conversation – think Enron, WorldCom, Madoff Securities, AIG. It is important to keep in mind that professionals like lawyers, engineers, and accountants are often willing participants in the fraud.

We mourn the pain inflicted on the average, everyday Americans who trusted these business leaders and professionals with their freedom, health, retirement money, etc. An angry public erupts again and again. Books and articles titled THE DECLINE OF ETHICAL BEHAVIOR IN BUSINESS[10] or THE SEVEN SIGNS OF ETHICAL

---

8   *See*, for example, Chris Matthews and Stephen Gandel, *The 5 Biggest Corporate Scandals of 2015*, FORTUNE MAGAZINE, December 27, 2015, http://fortune.com/2015/12/27/biggest-corporate-scandals-2015/.

9   For example, the state of Florida alone opened over 30,000 disciplinary files on lawyers accused of professional misconduct between 2011 and 2015. Many of these lawyers were vindicated and beat the charges. Some cases were dropped. Not all received discipline and Florida has over 100,000 licensed lawyers. Regardless, 30,000 is still a big number of violations deemed serious enough to open a file – especially for a cohort of people who passed their legal ethics class. See http://tinyurl.com/jk4w24m.

10   Jeffrey T. Luftig and Steven Ouellette, QUALITY DIGEST MAGAZINE, May 2, 2009.

Collapse[11] are written. Rules of Professional Conduct are tightened. Laws are passed with tough-sounding names like the *Sarbanes Oxley Accounting Reform and Investor Protection Act* (passed after major accounting scandals in 2002) and the *Dodd Frank Wall Street Reform and Consumer Protection Act* (passed after the 2008 financial crisis and real estate collapse).

These societal reactions are effective … to an extent. Some cheaters go to jail and even more lose their credentials, accreditation, and / or reputation. But others see their colleagues ensnared and find different ways to cross the line. Making matters worse, I believe a ton of unethical behavior goes undiscovered because cheaters are usually very good at hiding their tracks. No one wants to get caught breaking the rules and these bad actors are smart, highly-trained individuals. The watchdogs are generally budget-strapped organizations operating with limited resources and a huge herd to monitor. Here's the bottom line: the cheaters are generally slicker, faster, and more agile than the cheater catchers. Therefore, many perpetrators will remain free and fully licensed with the power to inflict great harm. This signals more pain on the horizon.

THE THREE ILLUSIONS OF ETHICS EDUCATION

So, why keep this struggling system in place, especially when it comes to something as important as ethics? The answer is simple: the status quo prevails because the professionals who run ethics education are amazingly risk adverse and resistant to change. It's difficult to get lawyers, doctors, accountants, professors, etc. to admit that what they have done over a career needs transformation. This is especially true if the people in charge of making the change, as well as the public at large, think the inculcation process is satisfactory. There are larger fish to fry, think drumming up business and increasing profit margins. Beyond their stubbornness, these people labor under three illusions that stifle change in the ethics education arena.

First, people believe that students who study professional standards in a rigorous classroom environment will care about their character enough to

---

11 Marianne Jennings, ST. MARTIN'S PRESS, 2006.

be good. In other words, placing rules and theories in front of students and requiring their attendance is enough to modify behavior. Hopefully, this chapter has already demonstrated this fallacy. Instead, the rules and theories must be buttressed with an actual desire and opportunity to overcome personal ethical dilemmas with integrity. This is what motivates buy in and behavioral change. With some tweaking, ethics classes can encourage this combination.

Second, people labor under the illusion that honor codes, core values, and mission statements are enough to cover the bases when it comes to ethics. The front page ethical meltdowns at some of our most prominent institutions prove this to be false. We will see that these institutions always have beautifully-written, highly-publicized values statements. Unless those in positions of power believe that their character matters, however, these values will not be sincerely held and rarely outweigh the perceived benefits of cutting corners.

Finally, people do not believe that ethics – in the character development sense – can be taught. They believe that individuals must come to these conclusions on their own (or with the help of a religious leader or wise family member) and that educators have no place in the process. Therefore, we waste time in seeking buy in and are better off sticking to rules of professional conduct. This is the easiest illusion to disprove. I will demonstrate how we consciously and subconsciously teach and learn about ethics from each other every day. If this is true, then we should all seek to be the best ethics teachers possible.

ILLUSION #1: STUDYING THEORIES & RULES IS ENOUGH TO CHANGE BEHAVIOR

I am a huge fan of education and believe most people should attend as many years of school as possible. Knowledge is power for sure. Education provides students with the toolkits and credibility to build long careers. A solid education with a focus on analytical, critical, and creative thinking is a must in today's ever-globalizing, complex world. It is common knowledge, however, that classroom environments struggle to help students effectively apply information to real-world circumstances. This makes classroom learning an incomplete vehicle to change behavior. Some schools are moving towards application or project-based education, but the results are mixed.[12] Much of life's most important lessons come outside of the classroom in the form of quality on-the-job training, life experience, and a desire to improve at one's craft. I call this disconnect the education-application gap.

For example, a Real Estate professor can cover a home purchase contract in depth, but comprehension of contractual nuances requires classroom knowledge as well as the representation of many parties in real-life transactions and an eagerness to master the process. A Graphic Design professor can test students on the ins and outs of Adobe Photoshop and Illustrator but, to improve, students need critiques of their work product by demanding clients as well as the desire to take constructive criticism to heart. The same analysis holds for ethics education. I can cover ethical decision-making frameworks until I am blue in the face and yet my students may still crumble if their boss asks them to choose between lying to a client or losing their job. My educational efforts alone, solid as they may be, are just not enough. Instead, my students must wrestle with ethical dilemmas in their lives outside the classroom and allow the often-painful outcomes fuel their desire to be better. Then and only then will they be more honest at work and resist the pull of unethical behavior. Therefore, ethics education stands by itself at one edge of the education-application gap.

But the lack of real world application does not mean that ethics education is useless. Below are two ways to teach ethics – the status quo ethics class and the transformational ethics class. We should transition from the former to the latter.

Status Quo Ethics Curriculum:

The curriculum of the typical ethics course makes it difficult for students to think about the things in life that make a person good – the real rabbits worth chasing. Take a legal ethics class, for example. Below is a smattering of the

---

12 Researchers have found that results of project-based learning are mixed. "Project-based learning is a teaching approach that engages students in sustained, collaborative real-world investigations. . . . Some studies suggest that it is an engaging instructional approach, but numerous studies have also claimed that students are not motivated by this type of learning, and that it places a great amount of stress on teachers." *See* Heather Coffey, *Project-Based Learning,* UNIVERSITY OF NORTH CAROLINA SCHOOL OF EDUCATION, http://www.learnnc.org/lp/pages/4753 (last visited December 30, 2016).

Professional Responsibility rules for lawyers. Play along and see if these rules in any way compel you to become a more moral person:

- It is professional misconduct for a lawyer to ... engage in conduct involving dishonesty, fraud, deceit or misrepresentation.[13]
- A lawyer shall not knowingly: make a false statement of fact or law to a tribunal or fail to correct a false statement of material fact or law previously made to the tribunal by the lawyer.[14]
- A lawyer shall not [as a condition of legal representation] require or demand sexual relations with any person.[15]

The words running through my head as we studied these rules were: "Duh," "Of course you cannot demand your client sleep with you in exchange for legal representation," "Wait, who wouldn't know that lying to a judge is bad?!" and "I cannot believe someone would be dumb and unethical enough to do these things." Did any of these rules catch you by surprise?

On and on the curriculum proceeds. I had not previously thought about 90% of the rules we went through in my ethics class. But, by semester's end, there was not one moment where I thought, "It's going to be really hard for me to be a lawyer now that I am forbidden to do this or that." The vast majority of this just naturally struck me as being obviously intuitive to anyone with any sort of moral compass or proper upbringing. None of these rules made me want to be a better person or treat people with respect, etc.

Again, other profession's rules of ethical conduct create similar and stunningly obvious restrictions. Here are some of their classic ethical no-nos:

- Accounting: A member shall be considered in violation of the [Code] if the member, by virtue of his or her negligence ... makes, or permits or directs another to make, materially false and misleading entries in the financial statements or records of an entity.[16] ... note: accounting fraud is bad! Got it.

---

13   Colorado Rules of Professional Conduct, Rule 8.4(c).
14   American Bar Association Model Rules of Professional Conduct, Rule 3.3(a)(1).
15   New York State Rules of Professional Conduct, Rule J(1)(i).
16   AICPA Code of Professional Conduct, Rule 1.400.040.01.

- Medicine: Sexual contact that occurs concurrent with the patient-physician relationship constitutes sexual misconduct.[17] ... note: no sex with patients, check!
- Finance: Members ... must understand and comply with all applicable laws, rules, and regulations ... of any government, regulatory organization, licensing agency, or professional association governing their professional activities.[18] ... note: merely complying with the rules now counts as ethical behavior!

Hopefully you can see that these should be the minimum standards of professional conduct. Again, none of this is bad. I agree with every one of these rules and you should too. I am glad that my doctor is forbidden from trading sexual favors for removing my gall bladder. I am relieved that accountants study the importance of accurate financial statements. However, little of this will make a person studying these rules say, "Wow! I really need to develop my character and become a better person so that I become a more ethical doctor or accountant." Yet this is what our world desperately needs. And, little of this should encourage the public that we are training ethical professionals. More likely, we are training people who are very good at complying with rules.

TRANSFORMATIONAL ETHICS CURRICULUM:

There is a better way. You can keep all the rules and theories mentioned above in the ethics class if you mix in some real-life character development and continually encourage buy in. Students should leave the class better morally than when they first enrolled. The problem is that this dual focus involves hard work, a lot of time, dedicated thought, uncomfortable behavior correction, and a large dose of humility by the teacher. But, it is possible to do well – I have boxes full of page-long thank you notes to prove it. Here is my approach.

I generally start with a group of students who are ambivalent or even angry that they must take an ethics class. This is typical and I'm not exactly preaching to the choir on the first day. But, I press on. I tell the Cash the Greyhound story right off the bat and refer to it every class session. I get personal and talk about

---

17   American Medical Association Code of Medical Ethics, Opinion 8.14.
18   Certified Financial Analyst Institute: Code of Ethics & Standards of Professional Conduct, Rule I(A).

how the story impacted my life, my career, and my marriage for the better. I tell students how I screwed up in the past. They love hearing these stories and it humanizes their professor. I distribute ten writing assignments where students must create a journal that tells me about situations where they acted unethically and how they think they should change their behavior (if at all). They are required to ponder their priorities, their chase of money, beauty, and popularity, and their virtues or lack thereof. They add to this journal all term until I collect a copy during the final.

For every reading on Kant or Aristotle, we have an equally powerful discussion of what it means to leave a legacy and be a role model. For every ethical framework we cover, we spend an equal amount of time talking about how to treat people well even when they cannot do anything for us or to us. The ethics class setting creates an environment where people are thinking about the right thing to do as they walk in the door each class. This should make it easier to have these tough conversations. I never force idea acceptance – that's the inculcation that doesn't work. I just plant seeds and encourage buy in. Students are perfectly free to tell me I'm full of it as long as they can justify their reasons. And some do. The vast majority, however, leave the class better morally than when they came in – and, that should be the goal of any ethics class. There is no reason that other professional ethics classes could not be similarly structured.

This information should make it hard for you to believe that Illusion #1 is widely accepted. But we continue to see ethics classes, credits, and certifications based solely on professional standards proliferate. These courses are generally required and tend to look and feel the same. Illusion #1 has convinced people that these ethics classes are good enough. They are not.

ILLUSION #2: WE HAVE HONOR CODES, MISSION STATEMENTS, AND CORE VALUES

Every university that has asked me to speak has an honor code. Every business (for profit or non-profit) and governmental entity that has asked me to speak has core values and a mission statement. I have seen many employees carry a small copy of their core values on laminated cards in their wallets; sometimes they do this willingly and sometimes it is required. These are beautifully written aspirations. You read these words and say, "Wow! I want to go to school or work at a place like this. I want to be a part of a group of people who feels this way and treats people this well." The problem with these statements is that they become meaningless manifestos if the people they govern are not much concerned about their character.

Let us pick on Honor Codes first. The typical university honor code is a product of the hard work of many people. These statements tend to be formulated by students, faculty, and administrators after months of research and committee work. They are usually well-written and often declare:

We the students promise not to cheat. This means we promise not to give or receive aid while taking examinations or writing essays. We promise not to improperly collaborate on assignments or submit the same piece of work in multiple classes. We abhor plagiarism and will submit work that is our own. We promise to hold ourselves to the highest standards of integrity and honesty as we undertake this educational journey. We also promise to report violations of this Honor Code, whether our own violations or those of our peers, to the Office of Student Conduct.

This is compelling. I love the wording. With honor codes like this you would assume that academic integrity beams from our institutions of higher education. The problem is that far less than half of American's college students consistently follow the honor code they promised to uphold. The statistics are shocking. In 2013, the Boston Globe wrote, "The rate of students who admit to cheating at least once in their college careers has held steady at somewhere around 75 percent since the first major survey on cheating in higher education in 1963."[19] In fact, seven out of every ten college students believe that most students cheat

---

19 James M. Lang, *How College Classes Encourage Cheating*, BOSTON GLOBE, August 4, 2013, http://tinyurl.com/guoqrq6.

at some point between freshman and senior year.[20] One researcher pegged the number at 68% after surveying over 71,000 undergraduates.[21] The number jumps to between 86% to 95% for high school students. It is within the realm of possibility that ninety-five percent of high school students cheat!

Studies show that today's students are more focused on grades than education and that, in the past, "it was the struggling student who was more likely to cheat just to get by. Today it is also the above-average college bound students who are cheating."[22] This level of cheating is remarkable and has forced me to completely retool the way I assess learning. I now teach what people call the "uncheatable ethics class."[23] It has a nice ring, but my class is part of a sad reality because my university also has what the public considers a strong honor code. The students even sign it before taking any classes. Making matters even worse, students are very reluctant to report cheating to their professors or the Office of Student Conduct – even though they promise to do so in the honor code they signed. They abstain because the negative reaction from their peers outweighs their honor code promises.

Let's bring these numbers outside the ivory tower. Can you imagine if any municipal law had a 70% violation rate? Take red light laws, for example. What if seven out of every ten drivers said, "Well, that red light just does not apply to me today; I'm in a hurry and I looked both ways," and randomly sped through stop lights. There would be chaos on the roads. People would be seriously hurt. What if 70% of people blew off the TSA checkpoints at airports thinking, "Well, I'm not a terrorist. I ditched all my liquids at the ticket counter. They can make

---

20 The data comes from students themselves as collected by the people who run major standardized tests. The Educational Testing Service along with the Ad Council created an *Academic Cheating Fact Sheet* which included these facts: "73% of all test takers, including prospective graduate students and teachers agree that most students do cheat at some point. 86% of high school students agreed." See http://tinyurl.com/5smux (ETS Study).

21 Dr. Donald McCabe, *Integrity: Statistics: Overview*, INTERNATIONAL CENTER FOR ACADEMIC INTEGRITY, http://www.academicintegrity.org/icai/integrity-3.php. After surveying over 70,000 high school students, Dr. McCabe pegged the high school cheating number at 95%.

22 ETS Study.

23 My classes are now all oral. 50% of a student's grade comes from a class participation score (so everyone must show up and talk for anyone's grade to be high) and the other 50% from a fifteen-minute, one-on-one oral final. This is officially an uncheatable class!

an exception for me today." Would you feel safe on your next flight? This would be dangerous and unfair. Students use similar faulty logic when they cheat and make justifications like, "Well, everyone else is doing it," "The professor didn't change the test," "College is expensive," "My parents will kill me if I don't make honor roll," and the classic "At least I am not cheating in a class for my major." It doesn't take a genius to realize that rules lose all meaning if they are violated 70% of the time.

This data and these justifications explain why I would rather universities purge their honor codes than allow them to be violated at such a high rate. This is all a result of universities handling academic integrity with inculcation versus buy in. As with ethics classes, the data proves that it is not working. You either follow the Code or get written up and maybe kicked out. You agree to the honor code so you can enroll in classes regardless of whether you agree with its terms. A better approach would be to seriously talk with first-year students about what it means to be a person of character and how cheating hurts them personally, is unfair to their peers, and damages society at large. Then have them sign the honor code. These are the conversations that should take place beginning at orientation and continuing throughout the college experience.

Now to core values and mission statements. Most are succinct and contain the word integrity (or a synonym for integrity). These are the commitments an organization makes to its employees and other stakeholders. They are also meant to comfort the public and to show the organization is on the right track. If your company has a set of these ethical proclamations, congratulations! You join a long a distinguished list of companies with publicized values, many who have recently crossed moral and legal boundaries. Here are but a few examples from the recent past: Enron, an oldie but goodie (classic accounting fraud), Mitsubishi (falsified fuel tests), Toshiba (fudged financial results to the tune of nearly $2 billion), Turing Pharmaceuticals (5,000% increase in drug prices for AIDS patients from $18 to $750 per pill) and Volkswagen (installed software that created false emissions readings). It is no surprise to me that each of these companies published core values that revolved around the word integrity. Here's a taste:

- ENRON | *Code of Ethics Manual* (a 64-page document by the way):
  - **Respect** – We treat others as we would like to be treated ourselves. We do not tolerate abusive or disrespectful treatment. Ruthlessness, callousness and arrogance don't belong here.
  - **Integrity** – We work with customers and prospects openly, honestly, and sincerely."[24]
- MITSUBISHI | Three Principles:
  - **Principle #2: Integrity and Fairness (*Shoji Komei*)** – Maintain principles of transparency and openness, conducting business with integrity and fairness.[25]
- TOSHIBA | Engineering Ethics:
  - **Corporate Policy** – Toshiba Group Companies shall … engage in technology activities with a high level of ethics.
  - **SOC for Toshiba Group Directors and Employees** – Directors and Employees shall: utilize their expertise, skills and experience to contribute to the health and happiness of humans and the safety of society.[26]
- TURING PHARMACEUTICALS | Global Code of Business Conduct:
  - **Message about the Purpose and Scope of the Code** – We expect all Turing employees to act with good faith and integrity. Acting with integrity means that we will: follow all the laws, regulations, and policies that impact our business operations. Treat each other and our customers and patients with the respect they deserve. Ask questions when unsure what to do in a particular situation.[27]
- VOLKSWAGEN | *Core Values*:

---

24 Uploaded by Bob Sutton: WORK MATTERS BLOG, http://bobsutton.typepad.com/files/enron-ethics.pdf (last viewed August 15, 2016).

25 *Three Principles*, MITSUBISHI WEBSITE, https://www.mitsubishi.com/e/history/principle.html (last viewed August 15, 2016).

26 *Toshiba Group Standards of Conduct*, TOSHIBA WEBSITE, http://www.toshiba.co.jp/csr/en/policy/soc.htm#SOC11 (last viewed August 15, 2016).

27 *Global Code of Business Conduct*, TURING PHARMACEUTICAL WEBPAGE, January 27, 2016, http://www.turingpharma.com/content/documents/20160127CodeOfConduct.pdf.

○ *Integrity* – Our everyday actions are based upon an internally-consistent framework of principles and values. We understand that integrity is more than just a word ... it is a daily practice.[28]

I could recite similar broken business promises all day long. The irony in some of this morally superior language is rich. I particularly love the concept of integrity as not just a word but a daily practice. This represents model behavior – in theory. What about the idea of providing patients the "respect they deserve" and then marking up a pill by 5,000%? Amazing. Please note that these ethics scandals are serious. This is not John thieving some money from the petty cash or Janet stealing an extra day of vacation and, thereby, violating the company's core values. Many of these examples are billion dollar frauds. Now you see why I don't place much stock in core values in and of themselves.

One final point should nail the coffin closed on this fallacy: If all these well-respected universities and corporations have these wonderful sounding honor codes and core values, how come so much serious unethical behavior continues to take place? I mean, many of these people carry these values on a business card in their wallets, how could they ever cheat? I'm kidding.

The answer, again, is painfully obvious. Students and employees need to buy in to honor codes and core values to make them effective. The people running Enron knew exactly what the words respect and integrity meant ... they just didn't care. These values meant less than increasing earnings and making a profit. These employees never truly bought into the ethics code their company promulgated. Students nationwide know exactly what their honor code prohibits, but something (high tuition, tough economy, peer pressure, or mad parents) always outweighs the code. Students just are not buying in to mandatory honor codes. And, organizations need to do much more to facilitate such buy in by allocating resources to critical conversations and culture change.

Problematically, this change is unlikely to happen because these organizational aspirations look so good on paper and in press releases. That explains why Illusion #2 has convinced the public that having core values, mission statements, and/or honor codes will suffice. They will not.

---

28 *Core Values*, VOLKSWAGEN INTERNATIONAL, INC. WEBPAGE, http://www.vwiinc.com/values/ (last visited August 15, 2016).

ILLUSION #3: YOU CAN'T TEACH CHARACTER

Illusion #3 boils down to the idea that it is impossible to teach someone else to be good. At best, you can only teach someone to follow professional ethical standards. Let us discuss this question early on so this fallacy does not linger in the back of your mind. This is by far the most frequent question an ethics professor is asked: can you really "teach" ethics? The skeptics point out that you cannot teach a colorblind person how to identify dark red on a painting. They insist that you cannot teach someone to have rhythm, apply common sense, or to be imaginative and funny. These are just qualities a person has or does not have. Bolstering their point, I just described how professional ethics classes by themselves lack the capacity to truly teach someone to be good. So, are these skeptics correct? Can ethics be taught?

My response is always: You can absolutely teach ethics! Where did you learn how to lie (everyone does)? Where did you learn to manipulate people, cheat, or gossip (most everyone has)? Where did you learn not to swear like a sailor around your grandmother (most people would not dare)? Where did you learn to treat people with respect, be dependable, and stand up against wrongdoing (most of us want to)?

We learn all this from the culture we live in, of course. In fact, we each teach and absorb ethics or the lack thereof from each other every day. In addition, we each have a conscience that analyzes our and others' actions and then identifies right from wrong. In summary, we learn how to be good from each other and from deep inside ourselves. So, yes you can teach ethics. What you cannot do, however, is force anyone to be good. That is all up to them. But, by teaching ethics the right way you can model behavior and plant some seeds that encourage others to be better.

So, there you have it. The CIOCCHETTI THEOREM demonstrating that personal ethics can indeed be taught. Elie Wiesel got it right: "We are all teachers, or should be. Anyone who relays experience to another person is a teacher." The secret is to talk about ethics in such a way that people buy into what you are selling. The rest of this book provides a roadmap for you to do just that.

Conclusion: The Ethics Inculcation Fire Drill

In the end, ethics inculcation resembles the fire drills we all hate. The classic fire drill is an example of required activity with little real world benefit. Events generally play out as follows: mandatory emergency preparedness memos are drafted and circulated. They are available for all to read, but almost nobody does. The fire department requires the alarm to sound once every six months or so. The people who hear it slowly finish what they were doing, gather their things, and slowly walk outside. It takes them forever. They then stand around shooting the breeze in a parking lot way too close to the building that is hypothetically on fire. Most are clueless as to where they should actually go or what they should actually do next. The rules tell them to stand there, so they do until someone tells them to move. Let's face it, fire drills are inconvenient and take up valuable time. The choice is simple, however – you go outside or you get in trouble.

The chances are high that people who experience a fire drill do not become more aware of the dangers of an actual fire or what to do when faced with this emergency. In fact, the continual drills may desensitize them to an actual fire alarm.[29] They go through the motions of the drill (doing most things all wrong) and then on with their lives. The whole process is designed to prod, scare, or coerce people into following the rules and thus prepare themselves for the emergency. No one doubts that the powers that be have the best of intentions. But, few people really buy in to the process because the requirements seem to be a waste of time.[30] It would be so much better to have your employees sit for ten minutes with someone who lost everything in a fire. Hearing that story would actually produce some buy in.

The fire drill problem depicts what often occurs with mandatory ethics training. The topic is important, but the process as currently configured is ineffective. Professionals with this type of training are not ready for the real-life

---

29 When was the last time you took a blasting car alarm seriously? Mine goes off when I hold my open trunk button too long. Truth be told; these are usually false alarms.
30 An article titled FIRE DRILLS ARE A WASTE OF TIME appeared online in a 2014 Campus Safety Magazine article. See http://www.campussafetymagazine.com/article/fire_drills_are_a_waste_of_time. The authors' point was that these drills aren't unnecessary, but ineffective in their current configuration.

ethical emergency. The education-application gap prevents such readiness. This is especially true when the rubber of a tough, unethical, cut throat world meets the road of ethics rules. It's easy to sit in a classroom, take notes, and provide the correct answer on a test (i.e., march outside for a drill). It's much harder to muster the courage to report accounting fraud or turn over hurtful evidence to the lawyers for your opponent (i.e., escape from a burning building).

This is because the ethics inculcation process does not require anyone to ponder the deep ethical questions that stumped me in my interview: Tell me why it matters to become a person of high moral character – at home and at work? What ethical decision making frameworks do you use and why do they matter? Why does your ability to be a moral actor make your employer, community, and world a better place? None of this makes you sit down and ponder whether you care about doing the right thing and why.

With all this mind, the following disclaimer should be signed by attendees at all mandatory ethics events, students receiving honor codes, and employees operating under core values:

I am about to attend a mandatory ethics class / be bound by a set of ethical standards. I understand that the actual desire to be a high character person is a prerequisite to absorbing something from this process. This curriculum may teach me about ethical rules and frameworks. These standards may provide the minimum ethical requirements of this organization, but they cannot, by themselves, make me an ethical _____ [insert: lawyer accountant, doctor, scientist, student, etc.]. For that I need to buy into the idea that being a high character person is something I desire to work diligently at, over time, in my life.

Please sign below:

X _____

I present this disclaimer to my students on the first day of their required ethics class. Now, they are on notice; there will be no attempt to inculcate ethics here. Rather, this is my attempt to get them to buy in. I tell them that this disclaimer is the "why" of the buy in process and that the "how" is up to them and the subject of the rest of this book. John Dewey's quote is prescient: "If we teach today as we taught yesterday, then we rob our children of tomorrow." It is no longer acceptable to just teach professional ethics classes and call it good. It is unrealistic and unfair to just expect people to pick the character and ethical decision making pieces up along their journey through life. Some may, most will not. We all have a responsibility to help future generations learn what being "good" truly means.

CHAPTER 3:

CHARACTER, COURAGE & CURVE BALLS

"You may encounter many defeats, but you must not be defeated. In fact, it may be necessary to encounter the defeats, so you can know who you are, what you can rise from, how you can still come out of it."
– Maya Angelou

"When life puts you in tough situations, Don't say, 'Why me,' say, 'Try me.'"
– unknown

A few things became clear as I walked off campus that beautiful, autumn afternoon. I botched the ethics questions - obviously. My meager responses left little doubt. It was not as if I gave so-so answers and moved on. I gave terrible answers and just sat there. I admitted that my character was an afterthought. I was more of a gut feeling guy, remember, busy developing other skills. I mentioned that winging ethical decisions produced good results in my life, but led to regret a bit too often. My approach made the consequences of my decisions tough to guesstimate. I just kept crossing my fingers, closing my eyes, and hoping for the best.

My inquisitor just sat there too – unimpressed to say the least. He wasn't happy about my "legal ethics class wasn't really about ethics" rationale for dodging his questions. He expected someone applying for this position to possess a well-contemplated philosophy about becoming a good human in a bad world. I sensed he had follow up inquiries. But, rather than allowing me to dig an even deeper hole, he ended early and walked me to my next appointment. We said goodbye and I sensed his relief as he walked away. I lost his vote. My next interviewer wasn't ready, so I gained a few moments to collect my thoughts.

WARNING: IGNORING YOUR CHARACTER MAY COST YOU A DREAM JOB

During my respite, I recalled an important rule of thumb for job interviews: Applicants who reply to character-focused questions with evasion, questionable answers, or lies are risky prospects. Savvy employers avoid them.[31] These candidates tend to fall into one of two categories: (1) the Moral Relativist who violates the rule of thumb on purpose and (2) the Deer in the Headlights whose cluelessness is to blame.

Both types tend to be bad for an employer who seeks to showcase integrity. I was aware of this rule of thumb and tried to avoid such a classification. But, everything happened so quickly. I am usually quick on my feet but, this day, I utterly failed to anticipate his questions and their depth. Clearly, I hadn't taken this area of my life seriously enough. Had I just talked myself out of the running for a dream job and into one of these suspect categories? Decide for yourself:

---

31 This rule of thumb is prominent in professional sports where teams are often torn between acquiring a superstar and potentially poisoning team culture with a bad apple. *See, for example,* Lindsey Young, *Zimmer, Spielman Wants High Character Players on Vikings' Roster,* MINNESOTA VIKINGS HOMEPAGE, March 2, 2016, available at http://tinyurl.com/jydoav5.

Category #1 | The Moral Relativist:

Some applicants evade ethics questions, lie, or answer them poorly because they don't value integrity as highly as society expects. These are not necessarily bad people. To them, character development is just not that big of a deal. They lean towards moral relativism which means they don't want you to judge them and, in turn, they won't judge you. To each his own. They evade because they want you to analyze their qualifications using the prerequisites, skills, and areas of expertise you posted in the job advertisement.

The problem is that employers who hire moral relativists run a high risk of contradicting their ethics pledges. I have yet to read a company mission statement that preaches, "Don't judge us on how we run our business and we won't judge you for the way you live your life. To this end, we seek to hire people with similar beliefs." That would be shocking. There would be calls for boycotts and divestitures. It's doubtful that customers, other employees, or the public would approve. Companies are not permitted to adopt moral relativism.

It can be tough to reject these candidates because many are supremely qualified in other important ways. Think of the many professional athletes on the market who boast significant talent but long rap sheets. They still find teams willing to take a chance. Sometimes the tradeoff works out, but often it ends in a public relations fiasco. Employers desperately seek to avoid fiascos of any sort. Therefore, unless you are super talented at your craft, adopting this ethical stance is likely to cost you. In most job situations, companies prefer to pass on overt moral relativists.

Fortunately, this group did not include me; I was a lot of things, but I was not a moral relativist.

Category #2 | The Deer in the Headlights:

And then there are the applicants who fumble ethics questions because they are genuinely puzzled by the topic. It's almost like they didn't expect questions on morality to come up. They freeze for a bit and then shoot from the hip, giving random answers on the fly. Bingo. This described me in my interview.

This group's ethical stance poses less of a risk to employers. For many legitimate reasons, they have not dedicated much time to thinking deeply about the idea of integrity. For instance, they may believe the topic is important (they aren't moral relativists), but their mind and time is focused elsewhere. There are diamonds in the rough in this category for sure – people who eventually buy in and become role models for everyone else. However, it takes plenty of resources to discover and develop these gems. Therefore, hiring people from this category is also a risky venture. Membership in this group may cost you a job as well.

From an employer perspective, classification of applicants into these two categories should make hiring decisions much easier, right? Avoid these people and just wait for applicants who care about their character to walk through the door. Risk avoidance complete. The problem with this conclusion is the dearth of qualified applicants who fall outside of these categories. There just are not a ton of people who think deeply enough about their character to ace the difficult ethics questions I was asked in my interview. Do you remember them? Would you be a Deer in the Headlights applicant as well?

- What does it mean to <u>you</u> to be a person of high moral character?
- What ethical decision-making approach do <u>you</u> utilize daily to grind through ethical grey areas?
- Are <u>you</u> a moral actor and, if so, why and how often?

Providing sophisticated answers on the spot is very difficult unless you've deeply analyzed this part of your life. In the end, most people flail here. That means that, sometimes, employers must take a chance on people to fill open positions and conduct business. Lucky for me. The moral of the story is that ignoring your character probably should cost you a job you desire. And, that's just the employment realm. A lack of character is also likely to seriously injure your relationships, reputation, and legacy.[32] It will also cause much disappointment.

WARNING: IGNORING YOUR CHARACTER MAY ALSO CAUSE DISAPPOINTMENT

The second thing that crystalized on my drive home was my disappointment. The idea of being a professor became compelling to me that day. Though teaching was far from my mind the week before, my time on campus was enlightening. These professors were influential figures in the community. They did interesting, interdisciplinary research and traveled the country propounding knowledge. They told stories of shaping young minds and orienting moral compasses towards the good. They had hundreds of thank you notes and relationships with former students to show for their efforts. I was impressed and thought back to my days as a student. I looked up to my professors and wished I could know half as much as they did. I wished I could discuss difficult subjects as fluently as they could. And, I discovered that these positions pay well and come with long summer and winter breaks. Being a college professor seemed like a loophole in life. I

---

32 For more on this issue, see Robert Hoyk and Paul Hersey, *The Ethical Executive: Becoming Aware of the Root Causes of Unethical Behavior,* STANFORD UNIVERSITY PRESS, April 7, 2010. To show the cost of unethical behavior, these authors placed an executive in a suit in handcuffs on the front cover.

crossed my fingers again and hoped my Deer in the Headlights posture would not disqualify me.

I also had a craving to use the intellectual side of my brain once more. Deep thinking pays enormous dividends and I wanted to ponder difficult questions every day. It was also time to improve my character and become an authentically good person. My shame from the interview prodded me to be better. Perhaps I could encourage young people to be better as well and then go out and do great things, the right way, with their lives. My little company helped people improve on the tennis court, but it didn't provide the time to make these commitments. I began to wonder whether my efforts would be more impactful in academia.

On the flip side. I was happy being the boss. Should I abandon this new business, give up my freedom, and work for someone else again? This was a conundrum. Almost home, the sun set along with my hopes for obtaining the professorship. My failure to articulate what character and integrity meant to me likely cost me a job opportunity I found compelling. I was disappointed and rightfully so. All of this even after having passed all my required ethics classes (that's a joke; see CHAPTER 2).

THE COURAGE TO HIT LIFE'S CURVE BALLS

Life has a way of throwing you a curve ball when you anticipate a fastball. This is inevitable so you might as well have an approach to your at-bats. A curve ball could take the form of a layoff, an unforeseen opportunity (in my case), a broken relationship, a potential new relationship, an unexpected financial loss, the death of someone you love, an unanticipated pregnancy, an accident, an uncomfortable but necessary confrontation, or a situation where you must fight for your life. You can't really plan for any of these things. They are just thrown at you unexpectedly.

The secret to a successful life is to hit some of the curves while others swing and miss. The ability to take advantage of life's curve balls is how you distance yourself from the crowd in a very positive way. Curve balls work because dilemmas create inflection points which force you to focus on what's important in life. I have many friends who blossomed after they got laid off, changed careers and made less money, divorced, beat cancer, or recovered from an addiction. The struggle sharpened their focus and they now thrive. They mustered the courage to "seek out the happiness in all of life's crappiness," so to speak.[33] I also know many people who continually miss their curve balls and struggle accordingly. They keep striking out, some of them without swinging at all.

I was about to receive another curve ball, a chance to redeem myself and focus my mind on doing something special with my life. My professor friend called me a week after my interview. He had good news. The department took a vote and many of them liked me. He was calling to offer me the job. I wanted to say, "How in the world did that happen? Did anyone else apply?" but I played it cool. I surmised that my presentation on law (my wife created awesome slides for me – don't tell anyone) combined with their desperation (that one professor just died, remember) earned me this chance.

A career in teaching was back on the table. But should I bite? This would be my third career change in as many years. Open the dictionary to "short-timer" and you should see my sheepish face smiling back at you with this annotation: *Short-Timer (noun): someone holding multiple jobs for less than a year each; see Corey Ciocchetti's career.* Lasting less than a year at subsequent jobs looks awful on a resume. In fact, for a young professional, this career trajectory is nearly as bad as getting fired three times in three years. You certainly have some explaining to do. I was apprehensive and a bit fearful. I went back and forth in my mind and asked around. Most thought I was nuts to start over again. The curve ball hurled my way. This job at DU would make me a better person – I would be immersed in analyzing the morality of my actions every day and have the chance to shape young minds – even though teaching was far from my comfort zone. The pros outweighed the cons. I decided to find the courage to dig in and swing.

I located a buyer for the tennis business on short notice and began to think about lesson plans instead of backhands. I was 27 years old and had never taught an academic class in my life. I had no formal training in pedagogy or PowerPoint. Before my very first class, my department chair looked at me and said, "You're in Room 200. There are forty sophomores in there. This ethics class is required so they probably don't want to be there. Good luck." That was it.

33 The origin of that saying is unknown.

No inspirational quotes or pats on the back. But, I walked into Room 200 with enthusiasm and an unending desire to figure it out. That has been my approach for over a decade. I am rarely the smartest person or hardest working person in any room on that campus. I don't have a lot of outside connections to boards of directors and CEOs and I hate to kiss up and hob knob. My secret to success is that I consistently persist at my goals with enthusiasm and unending desire to help students, further knowledge, and improve at my craft. When others quit, burn out, or move on, I just keep persisting towards my goals. Seven years after my interview, I received tenure and five years after that found myself promoted to department chair – of an ethics department mind you! I have encouraged thousands of students over the years thanks to my job at DU. I have spoken to hundreds of thousands of people in over forty states and two hundred cities about their character thanks to my job at DU. And, this book would not be in your hands without my job at DU. My life's foundation was built upon the opportunities this curve ball provided. I found my mark. Who knows where I would be today without taking the plunge.

My Theory on Life's Curve Balls

I found some courage, hit this curve ball, and discovered a purpose for my professional life. I also became a person who practices daily character improvement. This was something I needed desperately. Perhaps that's why the pitch was thrown to me at that moment? Who knows. Why particular events happen to specific people in life is above my pay grade. If I had that kind of insight, then I'd go to Vegas and bet on sports. I'd be rich … kidding! But, failing to know exactly why something happens to people doesn't mean you can't have a theory.

My theory continues to be that many of life's curve balls are thrown at you for a reason – to strengthen your character and/or move your life in a different direction. I look back on most of the curve balls thrown my way and can now see both reasons at work. That was certainly true with my new job. I was lukewarm morally and needed to become a better person. I was stagnant and needed to find my passion. My curveballs (quitting the law firm, starting and selling a brand-new business, choosing to be a teacher with no teaching experience) were catalysts that forced me to move.[34] I am much better for it. This all happened for these reasons. That's my theory at least and I'm sticking to it.

So, please do me two favors. First, permanently remove yourself from the Moral Relativist or Deer in the Headlights job applicant categories. Spend some quality time figuring out what character and integrity mean to you. Have a well-reasoned approach to tough ethical dilemmas other than crossing your fingers and going with your gut. Ponder why it matters to be a moral actor. Chances are you will be questioned on these issues at an inopportune time (i.e., a job interview or on a first date) where a poor answer can cost you dearly.

Second, adopt my theory on life's curveballs the next time you find yourself facing a difficult decision. Most people do not approach these situations with courage. So, they swing and miss or fail to swing at all. I want you to take a different approach. I want you to think hard about whether this opportunity can help you develop a stronger character or discover a passion – in other words, develop your foundation. Are you stagnant? Do you need a different motivation for your life or career path? Is it possible that this curve ball thrown your direction for a reason? If so, then muster the courage to swing like that pitch was intentionally thrown your way and that something wonderful might happen if you make contact.

---

34 I'm not sure the theory holds in all situations. Some curve balls are inexplicable even in hindsight. What character improvement comes when people get hit by cars or kids get cancer? Again, this is far above my pay grade and it breaks my heart to ponder. But, there is something to the idea that a character-building purpose lies behind many of life's curve balls and even a partial theory is better than no theory at all.

CHAPTER 4:

FAKE RABBITS

"I had been running & running all my life until I finally realized those rabbits I kept chasing weren't even real."
– Cash the Greyhound

"You can never get enough of what you don't need to make you happy."
– Eric Hoffer

"Fame is a vapor, popularity an accident, and riches take wings. Only one thing endures and that is character."
– Horace Greeley

THE GRAND FINALE: THE FABLE THAT CHANGED MY LIFE

We arrive at the grand finale of our (my) story. The first three chapters provide you with a mark to shoot for in life; in other words, a foundational place to dig deep and develop a strong character. CHAPTER 1 showcases the unexpected unhappiness that befalls people who build their foundation on a prestigious career with a high salary. They may get rich, but finding happiness is another matter entirely. This is an improper foundation to seek authentic happiness. I represent "Exhibit A", living proof that this approach rests on shaky ground. CHAPTER 2 expands on the idea that merely studying how to be a good person is insufficient for foundation building as well. You must first buy in and work hard at becoming a high character person. Then and only then are you positioned to be authentically happy. CHAPTER 3 demonstrates that: (1) a lack of character can cost you (a job at least and likely much more) and (2) constructing a foundation takes the courage to swing at some unexpected curve balls – especially those you believe can make you a better person.

There is just one more part of the story to tell and it is the most crucial. This chapter focuses on the idea that developing your foundation requires you to stop pursuing fake rabbits and begin to chase real rabbits. Buy in to this next part and you will find yourself equipped with the tools you need to find the happiness we all so desperately seek. And as a side benefit, once you do that, you can take all the ethics classes and be bound by all the honor codes you want. At that point, they might actually be helpful.

VOICES OF EXPERIENCE

My first class as a professor was a required ethics class – of course it was. And, as the department chairman told me on my first day on the job, the students really "didn't want to be there." I vowed to avoid the inculcation approach of read a book, listen to lecture, and take a few exams all to pass through some arbitrary ethics checkpoint. Instead, I was committed to inspiring my students to buy in to the importance of having character. Only then, would I be able to teach them in an environment where they would appreciate Aristotle and Kant. I had no idea how to do this mind you, but I was about to receive some serious inspiration.

At universities across the land, fliers litter classroom buildings. Hallways are full of colorful invitations that read: "Come hear the US Ambassador to Baghdad speak on Middle East politics," "Club Sports wants you to play Broomball," and "Career Fair on Thursday." It is hard to narrow down the relevant ones through all this noise. One winter day, however, someone posted their flyer in the men's restroom. That was smart as they certainly had a captive audience. It advertised a speaker series called Voices of Experience, featuring brilliant business minds who would inspire the next generation of business leaders. This flier had a picture of John Bogle. I knew his name as I had read his popular book called THE LITTLE BOOK OF COMMON SENSE INVESTING. John Bogle could claim much responsibility for inventing the low cost, low risk mutual fund.[35] This alternative allowed the average, middle class citizen a path to save for retirement with much less risk and confusion. FORTUNE MAGAZINE named him one of the four "investment giants" of the twentieth century.[36] He was coming to my campus to speak about business and he was a legend. I RSVP'd.

So did a ton of other people. The room was packed. Everyone wanted to hear John Bogle speak. I got there early and grabbed a seat in the front row. We all wanted to hear about the economy, job growth, and the investment climate. Mr. Bogle talked about some of that. But, near the end of his remarks, he stopped discussing business. He wanted to tell us all the secret to success in life via a soul-healing story about a dog. With this unexpected pivot, you could hear a pin drop. I had attended a lot of these events. The speakers stick to the script, take ten minutes of questions at the end, and exit stage left. These gigs are models of consistency. They NEVER venture off into stories about dogs. But, John Bogle was in his seventies and a multi-millionaire. What were people going to do … leave? There was no way. So, we all just sat there and listened to his story about the dog.

---

35   John Bogle marketed the first index mutual fund available to the general public – the Vanguard 500 Index Fund. Index funds invest in all or a select part of the stocks listed on a popular market index such as the S&P 500 or the NASDAQ. These funds are popular because they provide broad exposure to a market but operate at lower costs (they don't trade until the index changes) and lower risk (some diversify their risk by holding hundreds of stocks) than traditional index funds which trade in and out of individual stocks picked by the fund manager. *See Index Funds Could Help Lower Long-Term Costs*, VANGUARD HOME PAGE, http://tinyurl.com/krhrayx.

36   See Richard Loth, *The Greatest Investors: John (Jack) Bogle*, INVESTOPEDIA, http://tinyurl.com/z6dcsce.

He began to tell the tale of Cash the greyhound (return to the PREFACE and read it religiously; you should even print it and hang it on your fridge). He spoke slowly and articulately. He wanted to make sure we understood. As you now know, the story described Cash's critical analysis of his life and his subsequent relinquishment of a great deal of money and renown. It concludes with this wisdom:

> To the question of why he would leave it all behind in the peak of his career, Cash countered: "I've been pondering my life. After some critical reflection, it dawned on me that all I have ever done is run and run around these little oval, dirt tracks. That chase sums up my life, my identity. And, I finally discovered that, after all my efforts, those little white rabbits everyone, everywhere encourages me to chase. . . they aren't even real! I choose to step aside from this race and chase things that can make me happy.

The audience looked at each other. A few got it. They nodded and smiled. Someone said, "Amen." These were the people who had already bought in to their character development process. They were further along their journey to authentic success and probably would have aced the ethics interview questions. For them, John Bogle was preaching to the choir. The rest of us, however, just looked puzzled trying to figure it out. I remarked to the person next to me that the tale was "cute."

But, after a few minutes, a sinking feeling enveloped me. I thought about all the fake rabbits I chased to date. It was clear that none of them made me happy. I was just running and running around the track of life to no avail because that's what I saw others doing. I was just following the crowd. As he walked off stage, the last thing I heard John Bogle say was, "You can never get enough of what you don't need to make you happy." And like that, John Bogle was gone. And so was everyone else. Audience members gathered their things and headed for the exits. It was late.

I just sat there in the front row with my head in my hands thinking:

- Corey, you have more money than any of your friends;
- You have a better job and a more elite education than your peers;
- You have a nicer car and a bigger house than many people older than you;
- Your stuff is top of the line and you get to travel;
- People respect your accomplishments; so . . .
- <u>Why aren't you happy?</u>

This conversation troubled me. I had everything I ever wanted. As you know, I spent years of my life and many thousands of dollars to accumulate all this worldly success. The problem was that I possessed very little with the capacity to make me happy. I was chasing fake rabbits. I wanted to be rich. I wanted to be good looking. I wanted to be well-known and respected. I thought all this would make me happy. I worked very hard to achieve these goals yet I woke up every day unhappy and unsatisfied. I began to realize that MTV had lied to me!

THE WORLD IS LYING TO YOU!

I hope you realize that the world is lying to you too. Let me repeat: the world is lying to you! We are bombarded with messages that tell us to chase wealth, popularity, and fame. This all starts in school where we want to be popular and good-looking and continues through our careers where we combine those two fake rabbits with the desire to be rich. We look up to people in our communities who are sexy or skinny, people who are athletic or well-liked, people who live in the big houses or drive exotic cars. In our estimation, these attributes outweigh their character. Very rarely does someone say, "I really admire Mark down the street because he's a high character guy." Or, "I wish I could be as honest and compassionate as Sydney's mom."

Making matters worse, we encounter advertisements virtually everywhere that tell us to chase "the things that matter in life." We expect to then see a happy family or a group of friends – some of the things we cherish. But, instead, the commercial pans to an expensive sports car or a fancy outfit. And now we want one. We see social media posts of people on glamorous vacations or partying the night away and, now, we want to be there too. Our lives seem boring compared to their perfectly-posed adventures. It is impossible to compete with them because "we compare our behind-the-scenes with everyone else's highlight reel."[37] We see what they choose to post – the party, not the morning after hangover. We see them sipping champagne on the plane, not waiting for an hour in the TSA line. We forget that these people might not be all that happy either if they let us dig deep and verify.

But none of that seems to matter. We continue to chase mindlessly on our own little dirt track. We continue to find ourselves unhappy and wanting more of what we simply don't need. Maybe this time it will be different. When that doesn't happen, we eventually give up on that fake rabbit and chase another. It's a vicious cycle and one we participate in it all the time. We harbor thoughts such as: "Well I'll never be as rich as [insert the name of someone who may or may not be happy in the first place] in my neighborhood, but I sure do look sexier than she does in a dress." Or, "I'll never be as popular as [insert name of someone who may or may not be happy in the first place] at my school, but I'm much more athletic." Or, "I wish I was as pretty as [you know what goes here . . .], but I have a better job." This quickly becomes a game of one upping others, one fake rabbit after another. Again, I wish people would reverse their thinking and say, "I'll never be as rich as she is, but I am going to be the best parent I can be." Or, "I'll never be as popular as he is, but my goal is to plug in and make a few people a little happier."

On the evening of John Bogle's speech, I made the decision to chase real rabbits. I would spend some serious time and energy determining which things were worthy of my focus. Once this decision is made, the hard part begins. You must now consistently persist to stay on track as the world, including your friends, family, peers, and culture, try (often unwittingly) to push you off course. So, let's start with the easier part first – identifying and turning your focus away from what didn't work for me, the fake rabbits in life.

---

37   Steve Furtick – lead pastor at Elevation Church in Charlotte, North Carolina.

THE BIG THREE FAKE RABBITS: MONEY, BEAUTY & RENOWN

There are many fake rabbits – things lacking the capacity to make you happy no matter how much you accumulate. But pursuit of the Big Three – money, beauty, and renown – are the main unhappiness causers. Let me be clear: I recognize that there is nothing wrong with possessing any of these things *per se*. I don't want you to ignore these things and go chase real rabbits. Money is important. Looks build confidence. It feels good to have many people like you. The problem is that none of these things, in and of themselves, have the capacity to make a person authentically happy. Money cannot. If being wealthy made people happy, then why do we all know so many rich people who are miserable? Good looks cannot. If good looks could make a person happy, then why is it often true that the prettiest woman or most handsome man in any room is often the least content inside? Renown cannot. If renown could make a person happy, then why are so many so-called popular people (i.e., celebrities) consistently down in the dumps?

The reason is because these things always encourage people to long for more. Picture a gambler at a roulette table after she's lost her initial investment. She cannot leave because the jackpot is only one spin away. The goal is right in front of her in bright shiny lights. She exclaims, "Just one more spin, baby! Come on Double Zero. Ahhh, shoot … Red Seven. That cost me and someone else won big. But, that could have been me. Let's ante up and spin again!" We all strive to hit the jackpot from time to time. Sometimes we even compromise our values in the process. We then recognize that someone will always have more money, nicer stuff, turn more heads, or be more popular. Someone else seems to always be winning and happy. In the end, the whole adventure is downright discouraging. But it's tough to leave the table. That's where all the action is.

PEBBLE-SIZED HOLES

In the end, focusing on money, beauty, and renown to bring happiness is like trying to fill a bucket that has pebble-sized holes in the bottom … with pebbles. We drop in pebbles and wonder why our bucket stays empty. We get frustrated and gather more pebbles. We drop them in faster now and increase the quantity, but our bucket stays empty. We cannot win. We come to realize that the holes are permanent and this is the only bucket we get. Some pebbles remain with each pour. That's good because you'll need some to live a comfortable life. I'll reiterate: money is important to an extent, tending to your appearance is psychologically important, and it is reassuring to have people look up to you. But, the only way to fill your life to the brim is to drop in something with a little more substance. You need to fill your life with contentment, solid relationships, and a strong character – i.e., the real rabbits in life.

But, let's begin where the world encourages us to go – straight to the fake rabbits. It is time to tackle each of the Big Three individually and break some conventional wisdom. Read along and I bet we come to many of the same conclusions. The question is whether you can muster the courage to leave the table with the bright shiny lights and start filling your life with something more substantial.

CHAPTER 5:

MONEY

"There are people so poor that the only thing they have is money."
– Rodolfo Costa

*"The real measure of your wealth is how much you'd be worth
if you lost all your money."*
– Anonymous

Money isn't evil. In fact, accumulating money tends to be a good thing in and of itself. As George Bernard Shaw said, the "lack of money is the root of all evil." Rather, it is how we look at money and what we do with our money that brings unhappiness. It's good to have more than enough money to get by in the world. Life gets markedly less stressful when you do not have to worry about going to the grocery store or keeping the lights on. And life gets even easier when you have enough money to travel, retire comfortably, and pay for your children's college tuition. You could also argue that HIV and other world pandemics will eventually be cured primarily because of money – think of donations, scientist salaries, facilities, as well as drug invention and distribution.[38]

The academic studies back this up. Researchers at the University of Pennsylvania found money does make people happy – at least up until a certain level.[39] That level is a household income (two people's combined earnings) of $75,000. That means that the individual level is around $40,000 a year. So, every dollar you earn before you hit $40,000 makes you a lot happier. Past that point, it takes a lot more money to make a person even marginally happier. Each extra dollar buys less and less happiness. But we look up to people who make millions and often think, "I would be so happy with that income." Yes, you would be. Make no mistake about that. But, you would not be that much happier than if you made $960,000 less.

A different study makes a related point.[40] Researchers at the University of Michigan classified happiness into two categories: evaluative and affective. Evaluative happiness is "a sense that your life is good – you're satisfied with your life; you're progressing towards your life goals."[41] This is more of a look at a person's overall perspective on life. Affective happiness, on the other hand, looks at "how often you experience positive emotions like joy, affection, and tranquility, as opposed to negative ones."[42] This is more of a day-to-day happiness index. These researchers found that rich people have higher evaluative happiness than poor people and that, overall, people in rich countries are happier than people

---

38   The United States government's annual global HIV contribution is budgeted to be around $34 billion in 2017. *See U.S. Federal Funding for HIV/AIDS: Trends Over Time*, THE HENRY J. KAISER FAMILY FOUNDATION, June 10, 2016, http://tinyurl.com/hkv89uo.

39   Daniel Kahneman & Angus Deaton, Center for Health and Well-Being, Princeton University, *High Income Improves Evaluation of Life but not Emotional Well-Being*, PROCEEDINGS OF THE NATIONAL ACADEMY OF SCIENCES, August 4, 2010, http://tinyurl.com/h3qwbll.

40   Justin Wolfers & Betsey Stevenson, *Subjective Well-Being and Income: Is There Any Evidence of Satiation?* AMERICAN ECONOMIC REVIEW: PAPERS AND PROCEEDINGS, (2013) 103(3): 598-604, http://dx.doi.org/10.1257/aer.103.3.598.

41   Andrew Blackman, *Can Money Buy You Happiness?* WALL STREET JOURNAL, November 10, 2014, http://tinyurl.com/jqt2d7b.

42   Ibid.

who live in poor countries. But, affective happiness is different. It turns out that people with a lot of money do not necessarily have more affective happiness – more joy, affection, and tranquility than poorer people. So, it appears that you can be "satisfied with your life overall but you may not actually be happy at the [same] time."[43] The key is to achieve both forms of happiness and money can only get you part of the way home.

Finally, we need to talk about money's ability to buy stuff—the material things of life. A 2014 study by Professor Ryan Howell of San Francisco State University found that money can provide happiness but it depends upon how you spend it. It turns out that spending money on experiences makes people happier than spending money on material things. Well duh! This all makes perfect sense to me because these experiences generally happen with the people we love. We reminisce about some of them for decades. But people think the opposite. They load up on material things they think will last longer and provide greater happiness. The thought process is, "My new plasma television will last ten years, but my family reunion trip will last only a weekend. They both cost the same, but I can only buy one. I'll choose the television."

In this vein, Professor Howell found: People think material purchases offer better value for the money because experiences are fleeting, and material goods last longer. So, although they'll occasionally splurge on a big vacation or concert tickets, when they're in more money-conscious mode, they stick to material goods. But … when people looked back at their purchases, they realized that experiences actually provided better value.

"What we find is that there's this huge misforecast," he says. People think that experiences are only going to provide temporary happiness, but they actually provide both more happiness and

---

43   Ibid.

more lasting value." And yet we still keep on buying material things, because they're tangible and we think we can keep on using them.[44]

Making matters worse, people tend to adapt to their material things. This is why a new car or a new computer will make you happy for a little while and then the excitement fades. We get used to these things over time. This causes them to lose their happiness-producing vale. Amit Kumar (Cornell), Matthew Killingsworth (Berkeley) and Thomas Gilovich (Cornell) reached a similar conclusion.[45] "People often make a rational calculation: I have a limited amount of money, and I can either go there, or I can have this," Gilovich says. "If I go there, it'll be great, but it'll be done in no time. If I buy this thing, at least I'll always have it. That is factually true, but not psychologically true. We adapt to our material goods."[46] This is something these authors call Hedonic Adaptation – hedonic meaning physically pleasurable. We adapt to our new stuff and it doesn't provide the long-term pleasure we anticipated. Think about the last time you bought something expensive like a home, a car, or expensive jewelry. How long did that purchase make you happy? Surely it did for the day. But what about a week or a month? Probably not an entire year. These professors agree with the Experiences-Are-Better-Than-Stuff argument:

Experiences ... tend to meet more of our underlying psychological needs ... They're often shared with other people, giving us a greater sense of connection, and they form a bigger part of our sense of identity. If you've climbed in the Himalayas, that's something you'll always remember and talk about, long after all your favorite gadgets have gone to the landfill.[47]

44 Ibid.
45 Amit Kumar, Matthew A. Killingsworth & Thomas Gilovich, *Waiting for Merlot: Anticipatory Consumption of Experiential and Material Purchases*, PSYCHOLOGICAL SCIENCE, August 21, 2004, http://tinyurl.com/jzobyw2.
46 Ibid.
47 Ibid.

There you have it. The studies are in – from prestigious universities like Berkeley, Cornell, Michigan, and Penn. Combine these findings with a bit of common sense and you come to a few simple conclusions. First, money in and of itself is a very important thing … at least up until a certain point. That point appears to be less than $40,000 per person, per year. After that, it takes a lot more dollars to get the same happiness increase. Think of the things we sacrifice for money in order to achieve such small emotional gains. Second, money becomes destructive when it defines you. A French Proverb has it right: "Money is a good servant but a bad master." If the amount of money you make or have, or the clothes you wear, or the cars you drive define who you are as a person, then you've already lost. It's going to be tough to be truly happy with that mindset. Why? Because there will always be someone richer than you or with more stuff and nicer stuff than you. You will quickly adapt to your new stuff and want their stuff. Third, chasing money is something we do well in this country. We're taught to do it from childhood. We even have a term for the phenomenon – keeping up with the Joneses. There will always be a Jones family that has more than you do. Without the proper perspective on money, this reality means you will work very hard fruitlessly trying to fill your pebble-holed cup with even more pebbles. That, my friend, is a lost cause.

One final note. I keep coming back to this because this is where I start to lose people. Remember, you can still have nice things and be a wonderfully ethical person. You can still make a ton of money and have a rock-solid character. These things are not mutually exclusive and it is not helpful to think of money and morality in that way. For example, I still have my fancy car from my law firm days. It's getting old now and I will likely drive it until it gets too expensive to maintain. Then, I'll go buy another fancy car – maybe one that drives itself (kidding). I like nice cars; I have since I was little. And I can't say that getting a new sports car doesn't partially motivate my work ethic. It's okay to be partially motivated by money and the obtaining of nice things and fun, expensive experiences. Just don't let this stuff define who you are as a person. Don't hope that people value you because of what you have. If someone were to take my car away, I would still be me. That wasn't my outlook in the past. Now, however, what I drive does not define who I am or who I want to be in life. It adds nothing and takes nothing away from my foundation of character or my purpose. It's just a very nice car. It's a side pleasure, a fun preview before the feature film. You can have both money and nice stuff, but just make sure to prioritize contentment, relationships, and character much higher.

CHAPTER 6:

BEAUTY

"Mirrors lie. They don't show you what's inside."
– unknown

"Sometimes people are beautiful.
Not in looks.
Not in what they say.
Just in what they are."
– Markus Zusak, *I Am the Messenger*

It pays to be good looking. No really; good looking people get hired sooner, promoted more quickly, make more money, hold higher ranking positons, and are generally the last to be laid off.[48] Though being good looking does not raise your actual productivity, it does raise an employer's expectations that you will

---

48   Dario Maestripieri, *The Truth About Why Beautiful People Are More Successful,*
      PSYCHOLOGY TODAY: GAMES PRIMATES PLAY BLOG, March 8, 2012, http://
      tinyurl.com/z5hhbta.

do a better job.[49] On average, attractive people are paid over $230,000 more than unattractive people over a lifetime. It appears that employers believe that attractive people attract business.[50] And they just might. We are biologically drawn to attractive people and want to be around them. That could easily lead us to want to buy something from them or hire them for a project.

Amazingly, an expert in the area says that the only job where being ugly is an advantage is an armed robber! Professor Daniel Hamermesh from the University of London cites this sole counter example and states, "a study showing that if you commit armed robbery or theft, it pays to be uglier. The white-collar criminals are more successful if they are better-looking, but for crimes involving force, I'd rather be an ugly robber because I'd scare the guys and they'd give me their money faster."[51] That really tells you something about the way that most humans look at other people. Sadly, it turns out that many of us favor beautiful people. These facts allow us to surmise that being good looking clearly can help you earn more money in life. This is called the "Beauty Premium."[52]

The effectiveness of the Beauty Premium is deceiving when it comes to happiness. Research has shown that most of the happiness that comes from beauty is directly related to beautiful people making more money than their less attractive peers. Aside from money, there appears to be little inherent happiness gained from looks alone. Professor Hamermesh makes this point, "Personal beauty raises happiness. The majority of beauty's effect on happiness works through its impact on economic outcomes."[53]

But, we just learned that more money can increase only one form of happiness – your life satisfaction – and only to a point. Beyond that, the law of

49 *See*, for example, Markus M. Mobius (Harvard) and Tanya S. Rosenblat (Wesleyan), *Why beauty Matters*, AMERICAN ECONOMIC REVIEW, 96, no. 1: 222-235 (June 24, 2005), http://nrs.harvard.edu/urn-3:HUL.InstRepos:3043406. Apparently, this holds true even if you merely sound attractive on the phone.

50 *See* Daniel S. Hamermesh, *Beauty Pays: Why Attractive People Are More Successful*, PRINCETON UNIVERSITY PRESS, 2013. Professor Hamermesh is the founder of Pulchronomics - the economic study of beauty.

51 See Sue Shellenbarger, *On the Job, Beauty is More Than Skin Deep*, WALL STREET JOURNAL, October 27, 2011, http://tinyurl.com/zqf9uds.

52 See Drake Baer, *Scientists Identify 3 Reasons Why Attractive People Make More Money*, BUSINESS INSIDER MAGAZINE, November 10, 2014, http://tinyurl.com/lpqde7s.

53 *Beautiful People Are Happier, Economists Find*, UNIVERSITY OF TEXAS NEWS, Match 29, 2011, http://tinyurl.com/gpufdau.

diminishing returns kicks in and the satisfaction you gain with each dollar grows smaller. We also saw that earning more money has little effect on your ability to experience joy, affection, and tranquility. So, the Beauty Premium may make you incrementally happier with your station in life for a while, but it is unlikely to add more joy, affection, and tranquility in your life. We can turn this into an equation.

1. Good Looks = marginally more $$$ (3%-4% more a year than your peers);
2. More $$$ = more satisfaction with your place in the world ... to a point;
3. But, more $$$ ≠ more joy, affection & tranquility
4. So ... Good Looks = marginally more life satisfaction but ≠ more joy, affection & tranquility

Therefore, it appears that if you seek more joy, affection, and tranquility in your life (which is why you have this book, right?), the money increase from the Beauty Premium is basically irrelevant.

The Hedonic Adaptation is also in play with looks. Over time, you become used to how good looking you are and your beauty affects your happiness less and less. Now, you need people to think you look even more attractive than before in order to be happy. And on and on you chase. Well, becoming increasingly good looking is harder and harder to do especially as you age. Your face is your face and your body type is your body type. This at least partially explains why Americans spent $845 million on facelifts alone in 2010.[54] It's not just facelifts. The total number of cosmetic procedures in America has doubled since 2000 and over 15 million procedures were performed in 2015.[55] More than 4.7 million women in the United States have received breast augmentation since 1997.[56] Patients report short term satisfaction with the procedures. As time passes, however, the change has little or no effect on their self-esteem and does not remedy depression.[57] This is especially true with procedures performed on younger patients.[58] In fact, researchers find that cosmetic surgery does not increase satisfaction with one's appearance much in the long term and link many of these procedures to "increases in anxiety and depression, eating disorders, more alcohol use and more suicide attempts."[59] This does not mean that people should avoid cosmetic procedures if medically beneficial; that is an important conversation between you and your doctor. My point is just that plastic surgery is the wrong place to look for more happiness. Besides, chasing real rabbits is so much cheaper and less invasive.

And beauty backfires as soon as people find problems with your character. Have you ever noticed that even the most attractive people become more unattractive the more unethical they act? This quote makes this point beautifully (it focuses on women but applies equally to all):

54 Professor Hamermesh helps explain these high costs: "Like many other desirable commodities, beauty is scarce . . . and that scarcity commands a price." *See also* Abigail Tucker, *How Much Is Being Attractive Worth?* SMITHSONIAN MAGAZINE, November 2012, http://tinyurl.com/zawv9ob.

55 *American Society of Plastic Surgeons Releases Report Showing Shift in Procedures*, PLASTIC SURGERY.ORG, February 25, 2016, http://tinyurl.com/glmbrcw.

56 Mona Chalabi, Dear Mona, *What Percentage Of Women Have Breast Implants?* FIVE THIRTY EIGHT BLOG, October 30, 2014, http://tinyurl.com/nn6hc36.

57 See T. von Soest, I. L. Kvalem and L. Wichstrøm, *Predictors of Cosmetic Surgery and its Effects on Psychological Factors and Mental Health: A Population-Based Follow-Up Study among Norwegian Females*, PSYCHOLOGICAL MEDICINE, 42, pp 617-626, 2012.

58 Ibid.

59 Christian Jarrett, *Mental Health Problems Worsen After Cosmetic Surgery*, RESEARCH DIGEST, February 15, 2012, http://tinyurl.com/hfrk7xl (citing the Soest study).

Have you ever met a beautiful woman with a horrible personality? Upon meeting her, her beauty is extracted. Her hair is no longer silky, her face no longer perfect. Her lips don't entice you and her cheekbones don't excite you. Her skin doesn't glow and her eyes don't draw you in. It's a phenomenon that most people eventually experience, learning that an ugly soul can make the most beautiful face unattractive. And it holds true for the opposite of cases.

Souls radiate. They glow from the inside-out, making the most attractive people ugly and the prettiest faces unwanted. They turn men away and keep others running in the other direction. They turn first encounters into final meetings and second meetings into regrets. We've all experienced this firsthand, whether it was meeting men or women we once perceived as beautiful, only to find out they are people we don't care to know, or even look at, anymore.[60]

That's it – souls radiate and beauty fades with a lack of character (what the author of that quotation calls an ugly soul). I wish we would spend half the time beautifying our souls as we do our faces and bodies. Think of how much happier that would make us – our souls would shine brighter than our bodies. It is certainly true that beauty is only skin deep.

So, is it wrong from a moral standpoint to treat people better because of their looks? Is the Beauty Premium unethical? I think most deep thinking people would say yes. Favoring beauty certainly overlooks merit and the ethical norm of treating people equally. A beauty-centric culture causes people much pain and keeping up with the Joneses in terms of looks gets expensive. But, the Beauty Premium reflects human nature and it's not going to change anytime soon. It appears to be hard wired into our DNA. How do I know? I turn to my own unofficial data set and some research on envy.

---

60 Lauren Martin, *Why Being Happy Should Make You Beautiful And Not The Other Way Around*, ELITE DAILY, http://tinyurl.com/hdu7gz2.

I fly all the time – over 75,000 miles a year. That's a lot of plane rides and observing of my fellow passengers. I generally see one person reading the news or any type of book for every five people reading a celebrity gossip or fashion magazine. Those statistics aren't great for the future of America, but I get why the tabloids win. Gossip is much more leisurely and less excruciating reading than the news. Check out some of the headlines from recent tabloids:

- FSU Student Who Allegedly Tried to Eat Man's Face Drank Chemicals in Victim's Garage
- Meet Mr. Bagel, the World's Cutest Pet Chinchilla
- Tests Show It's Safer to Kiss Your Dog Than Your Significant Other
- Linda Thompson Talks SEX with Elvis – And Reveals He Had WHAT Done to His Face?![61]

Let's face it, these bylines compel you to want to read them – well, maybe not the one about sex with Elvis. I remain unconvinced that the excitement is the main reason why so many people are drawn to the tabloids. For some reason, we enjoy these stories because we take a certain amount of pleasure in Jennifer Aniston's pain. We tend to be a bit jealous and like to see good looking, rich celebrities knocked down a peg – especially when we think they deserved it or we are envious.[62] It's called schadenfreude. The problem is that envy doesn't make you any happier and is unethical under nearly every ethical framework. So yes, the way we treat people based on their looks – for better or worse – can be considered unethical. My advice is to push back against this inherent desire to judge people by their looks or misfortune because you certainly wouldn't want them to judge you that way. If you wouldn't want the Beauty Premium to negatively affect you, then put the tabloid down and pick up a newspaper.

61 PEOPLE MAGAZINE HOMEPAGE, http://www.people.com/people/ (viewed on August 23, 2016) and TMZ Homepage, (viewed on August 23, 2016).

62 See Mina Cikara (Carnegie Mellon) and Susan T. Fiske (Princeton), *Their Pain, Our Pleasure: Stereotype Content and Schadenfreude*, ANNALS OF THE NEW YORK ACADEMY OF SCIENCE, September 24, 2013, author manuscript available at http://www.ncbi.nlm.nih.gov/pmc/articles/PMC4472308/.

Beauty Is Skin Deep ... Duh!

Perhaps unsurprisingly, the result with good looks is the same as with money. Beauty just does not have the capacity, in and of itself, to make a person happy. By trying to fill your cups with the endless pursuit of the perfect body, face, or looks you are just wasting your pebbles. That doesn't mean you should neglect your appearance. By all means, you should try to be good looking. Good looks build your confidence and confident people are happier people. Be good looking because it makes you feel better about yourself and not because others will look at you approvingly. Take advantage of the Beauty Premium and make more money since humans will always care about looks. But, as with money, the secret is to never let your appearance define who you are. That's a job for your soul!

In conclusion, perhaps it would be helpful to keep this quote in mind as you ponder your looks: "A pretty face gets old. A nice body will change. But a good person will always be a good person."[63] This is basically a longer version of what your grandmother always told you – it's what's on the inside that really matters. Grandmas are so smart!

---

63   Attributed to Olubayo Adebiyi and adapted by me to apply to both sexes.

CHAPTER 7:

Popularity & Renown

"If you have friends who actually like you, you are popular enough."
– E. Lockhart

"Fame means millions of people have the wrong idea of who you are."
– Erica Jong

We conclude our fake-rabbit trilogy by returning to high school. Yes, high school. This will be an uncomfortable reunion of sorts. Just bite the bullet and force yourself to recall what you chased during those formative years. I am aware that many of you soundly discarded that set of memories long ago. Me too. For most, high school is not our finest hour and that is probably a good thing. We have a lot more life to live and the journey becomes more meaningful as we mature. But that doesn't address the question as to why high school is particularly painful for most people? One answer revolves around the glorification of our third fake rabbit: Popularity & Renown.

THE POPULARITY PARADOX

Many high school students find themselves immersed in what I call the Popularity Paradox. They dedicate precious time and energy to become popular. It dominates their thoughts; they employ all superficial means at their disposal to reach this goal. They bad mouth friends to other friends, they make reckless choices, they dress provocatively, they cheat, they calculate who to hang out with. Most of this lies outside of their comfort zone, but it's part of the ritual. Upon becoming popular, however, young people become disappointed that their popularity is not providing the abundant happiness previously envisioned. Everything turns out so differently in the movies.

This hunt for popularity is not just some disorganized episode that rears its ugly head from time to time when the environment is ripe. It is just the opposite. The typical high school popularity contest is a well-oiled machine with orderly rules and complex social norms. It is grafted into high school culture across the land and inherited from generation to generation. The machine encourages an all-out sprint straight to a dead end. The race often devolves into ostracizing, bullying, and violence – sometimes employed by the popular kids but oftentimes used against them when their status changes.[64]

The Popularity Paradox is relatively simple to express but much more difficult to remedy. Because we adults are unsure on how to slow it down, we allow these popularity contests to march on at the expense of meeting the most critical objectives of high school. I do not mean to criticize education-based legislation or lesson plans *per se* (at least in this forum). Instead, I am critical of the lack of focus – at home, at school, and in our communities – on encouraging these vulnerable young people to develop their moral compasses. In our confusion, we turn a blind eye to a fundamental truth of human nature – young people with limited attention spans and life experience will tend to focus on popularity at the expense of character. This is what they see from others in popular culture where

---

64 "For many teenagers navigating the social challenges of high school, the ultimate goal is to become part of the 'popular' crowd. But new research suggests that the road to high school popularity can be treacherous, and that students near the top of the social hierarchy are often both perpetrators and victims of aggressive behavior involving their peers." Stuart Bradford, *Web of Popularity, Achieved by Bullying*, NEW YORK TIMES, February 14, 2011, http://tinyurl.com/zrb6qye.

the chase of popularity is much sexier than school. So, we allow the machine to operate without putting up an effective counter-attack.

But we should never forget that a young person with character will morph into a student who focuses on more substantive goals. And this is exactly the type of child we desire, the type of student our schools need, and the type of person our communities desperately seek to employ. There is little doubt that high character students are more likely to: (1) approach their education with the required diligence, (2) create a fairer academic community, (3) adhere to moral norms and stay out of (as much) trouble at home and at school, (4) act as role models to other impressionable young people, and (5) seek some real friends with stronger moral compasses. The reality is that high character students thrive. And we seem willing to sacrifice much of this potential to the popularity machine by not speaking up and encouraging a different path.

TOUGH CUSTOMERS

I get invited to speak at high schools all the time. It's an honor but, make no mistake about it, these are my toughest customers. Anywhere else, I tend to receive a warm and engaged audience, genuine laughter, and even a standing ovation from time to time. But, this rarely happens at a high school. The culture pushes back hard against my message. It starts when I am introduced at the required assembly and continues until the bell rings. I wouldn't dare do Q&A at one of these events. I would hear crickets and then maybe one teacher would bail me out with a lame question … maybe. There is a lot of thinking going on but it's not the productive kind I seek. It's more of the, "This speaker is funny, but is it cool to laugh at this guy's jokes?" or "If it looks like I am listening to him people will mock me so, I'll close my eyes and sleep" or "I can't wait to tell Hailey that Jake was hungover on the bus this morning!"

I take the stage anyway and try to make an impact. And I can. Inevitably, after my talk, many kids come up to say thanks. We talk and take pictures. There are some sweet young people full of potential in our high schools. A few of the popular kids also find their way into the line. These students, however, want to talk in private. We walk to a quiet place and they whisper some version of the Popularity Paradox. In their words:

Thank you for coming and saying all this. My school really needed to hear it. I guess I am now embarrassed to say that I am one of the most popular people here. What you said really got to me. I'm popular for all the wrong reasons – i.e., I have access to alcohol, I sleep around, I have a fancy car, I'm on the football team, I'm a cheerleader, I good at making fun of other people, or [insert another superficial reason for being popular]. But, I'm really unhappy most of the time. I go home and I'm depressed or enraged. I have a hard time getting up in the morning and doing this all over again.

If people got to know who I am, they wouldn't want anything to do with me. And, they certainly wouldn't follow me. But, I guess it's better to be popular. I get invited to all the parties and I always have a date. My phone blows up and people do me all kinds of favors. Life is just less stressful this way, I guess. I'm not sure the other popular kids were really listening to what you said, they were texting. But they need to hear this because my experience is their experience as well. Anyway ... thanks for coming.

These are heartbreaking conversations. They have cost me many a night's sleep. Some of these students leave in tears. It's amazing to me how deeply these young people have thought about this dilemma. It sounds like they would be happy to move cross country and change schools. I guess I would too if I were in their shoes. It would be hard to show up in the morning to a place where people adore me for superficial reasons and, at the same time, where I dislike who I am as a person.

WHAT DOES THE DATA SAY?

I've touched on the idea that our high schools exist to prepare young people to become college and career ready, to develop socially, to plug into their community, and to find a few life-long friends. Little of this is happening. Instead of encouraging this healthy educational and emotional growth, students seek to become as popular as possible and retain such status for as long as possible. Popularity trumps all.

And the academic studies back me up. Experts find that high schools, though improving, still struggle to meet educational goals. Due to what is often characterized as a leaky educational pipeline, "too many students fail to complete high school and make a <u>successful</u> transition to postsecondary education and careers."[65] 80% of high school students graduate, a solid number and a big increase from the past, but "less than half of those are able to proficiently read or complete math problems."[66] Remarkably, these students are "passed on to the next grade when they should be held back, and then they are unable to complete grade-level work and keep up with their classmates."[67] More and more students receive diplomas but most high school graduates are ill prepared for the bigger stage of life.

High schools also struggle to create student cultures of emotional stability and happiness. A study of 22,000 high school students by faculty at Yale University concluded that the "message is clear: our high schoolers are none too happy, at least when they're in school."[68] Students report feeling tired, stressed, and bored; a whopping 75% of the words they use to describe how they feel in

---

65 Michael Bangser, *Preparing High School Students for Successful Transitions to Postsecondary Education and Employment,* NATIONAL HIGH SCHOOL CENTER, August 2008, http://tinyurl.com/hx66svj.

66 Matthew Lynch, *10 Reasons the U.S. Education System is Failing,* EDUCATION WEEK, August 27, 2015, http://tinyurl.com/hlr4pdw. Much of this information comes from the National Assessment of Educational Progress – the largest standardized test administered in the United States.

67 Ibid.

68 This is all discussed on YALE CENTER FOR EMOTIONAL INTELLIGENCE'S HOMEPAGE, *The Emotion Revolution,* http://ei.yale.edu/what-we-do/emotion-revolution/ (last visited August 24, 2016).

school are negative.[69] Only 22% identified as "happy" but, when asked how they wanted to feel they said, "Happy, Energized and Excited."[70]

And, the so-called cool kids are more likely to have more serious trouble later in life than their less popular counterparts. One study by University of Virginia researchers – aptly titled *Whatever Happened to the "Cool" Kids?* – surveyed popular students ten years removed from middle school. They found that the former "cool kids" used 40% more drugs and alcohol and were over 20% more likely to run into legal trouble.[71] Their social competence – how well they currently get along with friends, acquaintances, and romantic partners – was 24% lower than their less popular counterparts.[72] The lead author of the study made a fitting observation:

You see the person who was cool ... [the person who] did exciting things that were intimidating and seemed glamorous at the time and then five or 10 years later, they are working in a menial job and have poor relationships and such, and the other kid who was quiet and had good friends but didn't really attract much attention and was a little intimidated is doing great. It's ... revenge of the quiet, good kids.[73]

Let me get this straight; our young students desperately want to be happy, energized, and excited but three fourths of the words they use to describe their existence in high school are negative?! And, ten years later, those in the popular crowd are more likely to be in trouble with the law, involved with more drugs

---

69   Ibid.
70   Ibid.
71   Joseph P. Allen, Megan M. Schad, Barbara Oudekerk & Joanna Chango, *Whatever Happened to the "Cool" Kids? Long-Term Sequelae of Early Adolescent Pseudomature Behavior*, CHILD DEVELOPMENT, June 11, 2014, available for a fee at http://tinyurl.com/hkx9v4q.
72   Ibid.
73   Kelly Wallace, *Cool Kids Study Offers "Revenge" For Nerds*, CNN, June 20, 2014, http://tinyurl.com/gopou6e (statement of Joseph Allen).

and alcohol, and have lower social competence? I am sure you sense the irony of the Popularity Paradox at work here.

As you can see, my conversations with high school students dovetail nicely with the data and show that these so-called popular kids aren't all that happy. From the manner it is portrayed in our culture, however, one would think that such popularity would bring much happiness at present and later in life. These kids are looked up to, they get to go to all the parties, they always have a date to prom or the football game. The stuff that makes them so popular will only grow over time, right? The reality is just the opposite. By now, you know why. Popularity, like money and good looks, just does not have the capacity to make a person authentically happy. Something must change.

As with the other fake rabbits, people adapt to their popularity and become desensitized. They keep chasing this fake rabbit, however, because popularity is what the world tells them to chase. They don't want to feel ostracized by publically taking a different approach to life. And they justify the decisions to me by saying, "Life is just less stressful this way, I guess" But that's wrong. In reality, people become less and less happy this way because their attention and energy becomes diverted from the things that really matter. These kids need our help and encouragement. We know popularity won't make them happy and now we need to say so!

P.S. – THERE'S NOTHING WRONG WITH STUDENTS BEING POPULAR

Finally, it seems important to note yet again that this is not breaking news and there is nothing wrong with being popular. I'm sure the Popularity Paradox was an issue in America's first high schools. Being well-liked is a very good thing. The problem is that popularity is defining these kids' existence and this ensures that they chase this fake rabbit at the expense of substantive goals. Why would we settle for a system where nearly eight out of every ten of our teenagers are unhappy in the place where they spend most of their formative years? How can we allow this culture to go virtually unchecked while less than half of our graduates cannot effectively read and do math? I argue that the blame falls on all of us – parents, teachers, administrators, and concerned citizens, the stakeholders in these kids' lives, for not focusing more attention on what they chase. It isn't fair to pin all this on generation after generation of sixteen to eighteen year olds – they are just following our lead. We have established a culture where chasing this fake rabbit is tolerated and often glamorized.

My Proposed Solution

You might counter with a list of the many groups with resources dedicated to bullying prevention, or sexual assault prevention, or curbing substance abuse in our high schools. I am aware of and commend this hard work.

As a parent of two precious daughters, let me say, **"Thank You!"**

My argument is not with these groups or their efforts. Rather, I disagree with the order in which we attack these problems. The current approach focuses on the consequences of bad behavior (i.e., bullying, sexual assault, substance abuse) where we would be better off going to the source – the character of our students or lack thereof. To me, it's less effective to tackle bullying in our schools than it is to motivate character. High character individuals don't bully. It's less effective to tackle sexual assault prevention than it is to motivate character. High character people don't commit sexual assaults. And, a community of high character individuals protects and looks after each other. These communities are something we sorely lack and their absence stands out whenever am I asked to speak after another sexual assault occurs at another educational institution. The same is true for serious underage drinking and drug use and on down the list of high school problems. The current approach is failing and it is past time to try something different. Let's start encouraging these popular kids to chase more contentment in their lives, a smaller group of real friends who like them for the right reasons, and a solid character.

And, by encouraging young people, I mean let's dedicate our resources and role models, our time and attention. We don't need experts here – just smart, moral people trying to do the right thing. Why not unleash our dedicated high school teachers to reflect with their students on what it means to lead an ethical life? This doesn't have to be expensive either. Wouldn't you volunteer to talk to a kid about character in an after-school program a few times a month? And I bet you know five other people who would do the same. So, round them up and call the principal at your local high school. Ask to start a Real Rabbits mentoring program. What administrator would say no to a group of concerned citizens (you don't have to be a parent) talking to students for free about becoming good people. We must attack this problem from its source and delegitimize the fake rabbits our students chase – our future literally depends on it.

RENOWN: THE ADULT VERSION OF BEING COOL

Let's move past high school to the adult realm. People in these more mature stages of life tend to move away from the popularity chase. Most of my college students couldn't care less about their popularity status. Their community is much bigger and more spread out than a high school campus. Unlike a typical high school, it's hard for college students to even know who's who on campus as they break off into different programs and majors. The same is true for adults in the working world. How would you even know who was popular in the office building next to yours?

What people start to look for at this point is RENOWN: the desire to be talked about by many people, to be well-known, to be famous. Renown is like popularity in that it still requires a lot of people to look up to you. It can also involve the chasing of some fake rabbits. Think about your average reality television star running around half naked seeking a huge cash payout or a marriage! Renown is also bit different from popularity because the target is so much wider. In high school, you tend to be popular if you are good looking, appropriately dressed, athletic, or a bit reckless. In the adult world, all those things count plus money, a prestigious job, and the ability to lord power over others at work or in the community, etc. There are many more ways to gain renown and that makes matters worse.

It should come as no surprise that renown also lacks the capacity, in and of itself, to make a person happy. As with popularity, the opposite tends to be true. The best place to start making some comparisons is with most famous group – our celebrities.

CELEBRITY & FAME

Think about the celebrity life. Imagine being mobbed by adoring fans, chased by paparazzi taking pictures of your clothes and hairstyle, making more money than entire extended families combined, and partaking in experiences that the rest of us cannot access. You travel by private jet, get invited to celebrity-only rooms, and sit in VIP seats at the Super Bowl. Sounds amazing, right? Perhaps it's ironic then that so many celebrities talk about how they wish they weren't so famous. They desperately want more privacy and many aspire to be more authentic and less of what the world wants them to be.

A telling example of this paradox is Pat O'Brien. Mr. O'Brien was once a Hollywood interviewer and bona fide celebrity himself before a very public downfall attributable to alcoholism and a phone sex scandal. At his peak, he wore $3,000 custom-tailored suits accented with gold and silver cuff links and $500 ties; he was driven to work in his black Maserati where he had two dressing rooms full of people to help him look his best.[74] In a post-rehab interview with Oprah, he courageously discussed his fall from fame and the idea that being a celebrity had little to do with his happiness. He made the remarkable statement that very few celebrities are authentically happy:

---

74   Sherryl Connelly, *'The Insider' host Pat O'Brien Recounts Rise to Celebrity Fame, Battle with Alcohol Addiction in New Memoir*, NEW YORK DAILY NEWS, August 2, 2014, http://tinyurl.com/k5gl2xa.

The thing about "fame" is that we are people who love to be loved by strangers ... We can't get enough ... You want more, more, more. The only number you have is "more." And I think of famous people ... I can name, out of all of them, 10 really happy ones[75].

One reporter covered his story, and celebrity downfalls more broadly, and aptly wrote: "But then the insatiable thirst for adoration becomes a void in which many celebrities find themselves lost, battling against unhappiness. [But,] the truly happy celebrities have figured out something very important about not just their star status, but life in general."[76] Indeed. Anyone want to guess what that very important "something" is that the happiest celebrities have figured out? The reporter doesn't say, but my guess is that it has to do with chasing real rabbits.

The problem with fame not equating to happiness is widespread. The UK-based Marriage Foundation claims that celebrity marriages are twice as likely to end in divorce (40%) in ten years compared to the rest of us (20%).[77] Statistics also show that celebrities die thirteen years earlier than the average American and are four times more likely to commit suicide.[78] These are shocking numbers that provide a powerful warning. A prominent family law judge in England summed it up well, "The worrying feature of these statistics is the picture they paint to those who regard the celebrity lifestyle as something to be admired and copied for its own sake ... These are, after all, the role models upon which many, especially young people, fashion their lives. Aspiration for happiness built on celebrity lifestyle is, it seems, dangerously flawed."[79]

---

75 *Pat O'Brien Explains Why So Many Celebrities Aren't Truly Happy*, HUFFINGTON POST, August 27, 2014, http://tinyurl.com/jk9guva.

76 Ibid.

77 *See* Steve Doughty, *Celebrities are Less Happy Than the Rest of Us Says Top Divorce Judge*, UK DAILY MAIL, November 18, 2012, http://tinyurl.com/j9cltuj (hereinafter Celebrities Are Less Happy).

78 *See* Kevin O'Keefe, *An Average Surprise*, NEW YORK TIMES: OPINION PAGE, November 12, 2006, http://tinyurl.com/h4wx6yb.

79 Celebrities Are Less Happy.

THE LESS FAMOUS, BUT STILL WELL-KNOWN CROWD

Let's move down the chain a bit. We have seen that fame does not make our top celebrities all that happy – it might even shorten their lives. But, what about less famous, but still well-known people? These are people that don't have to shake paparazzi or worry about what's going on in the VIP section of the club – they can't get in. But, they live newsworthy lives and people want to know more about them. In this group are our major executives, authors, entrepreneurs, (some) professional speakers, and (most) politicians. Their situation is different, right? They are happier with their renown because it doesn't come with all the trappings of celebrity, right? Well, yes and no. I'll explain.

Most of us want to make an impact in our world, to do something newsworthy. Making a difference is a huge part of what turns a job into a fulfilling career. We also want to see our hard work rewarded with recognition, it's good for morale. Our efforts somehow seem less important if no one notices them. That perception, of course, is nonsense. For example, people who endow university scholarships anonymously have done as much good as any public donation of the same amount. The inability to recognize donors by name takes nothing away from the impact of their benevolence. The ability of renown to bring happiness boils down to your intent – the "why" that motivates your actions. There are two types of relevant intent: (1) an intent to become renowned and (2) an intent to make an impact.

You stand little chance of your actions making you happy if you act merely for the sake of having more people look up to or like you, in other words, if you goal is to become renowned. People act with this intent all the time – *see* reality television or provocative news commentary. Both are intended more to generate renown than make a point. You certainly may find success in this realm and accumulate many admirers. But, the next time you take this approach think about the following study. A group of researchers studied over 16,000 people over four years. They found that the people with more renown – those who added more and more friends and admirers - became less sociable, more introverted, and experienced increased sadness.[80] This happens because being so well-known makes you neglect the formation of new relationships; this neglect then makes you sad. So, seeking renown for its own sake has negative repercussions.

On the other hand, acting to make an impact will produce much more happiness. Here, your intent is pure. If you do impactful things primarily for the sake of doing impactful things and you also get recognized, that's different. Renown based on this intention might actually make you happy. Why? At this point, you are not seeking the spotlight and are better able to avoid the trappings of trying to satisfy so many people. Your being isn't affected by whether the number who like you grows, drops, or stays stagnant.

With all this in mind, here is our equation for fame and renown as they relate to happiness:

1. Fame & Renown (for its own sake) = More $$$, access & unique experiences, which = marginally more life satisfaction; BUT
2. Fame & Renown (for its own sake) ≠ affective happiness (joy, affection, and tranquility), may increase introversion and sadness, may decrease sociability, and might even shorten your life.

These aren't the type of math equations that work in your favor very often. This is because the same logic holds for adults seeking renown as it does for celebrities seeking fame and students seeking to be popular. Apparently, you just can't get enough of any of this to truly make you happy. The Real Rabbits theory wins again. So, here's the balance you should strike. Seek to be well-liked and respected – at home and at work. These pats on the back build confidence and motivate us to be better and work harder. Being liked by more people widens our social network when we need to call upon an expert for advice or a friend for help. Everyone appreciates the morale boost that recognition provides. Do you hear that bosses? Pat your good people on the back more often. It builds morale and it's free. In the end, it's just good business to be well liked. Let's face it:

---

80 Christopher J. Soto, *Is Happiness Good for Your Personality? Concurrent and Prospective Relations of the Big Five with Subjective Well-Being*, JOURNAL OF PERSONALITY, Volume 83, Issue I, pages 45-55, February 2015, available for a fee at http://tinyurl.com/hvcefe4.

> *People become loyal customers because they like you. Customers forgive mistakes because they like you. Employees stay with you because they like you. Bankers lend you money because they like you. Vendors extend you credit because they like you. Being well-liked can do a lot for you.*[81]

The secret is to avoid <u>seeking</u> popularity, fame, or renown for their own sake. These things remain morally neutral until they start to define your life. If you look at them as a side benefit to the impactful work you accomplish, however, then you won't have a problem. Just make sure your intent (heart) is in the right place. And, don't confuse popularity, fame or renown (all fake rabbits) with real friendships (one of the three real rabbits). You absolutely need a few strong friendships in your life. More on the importance of solid relationships in CHAPTER 9.

BUT ... I LIKE MONEY, GOOD LOOKS, AND POPULARITY / RENOWN

Believe me, I know this – I've met a lot of you. I like money, good looks, and renown too. But I think the possession of these fake rabbits can be reconciled with an authentic life. If money or good looks or popularity come with your chase, then that's great. There is no need to shy away. This isn't one of those books that tells you to be poor or ugly or hermitish to be happy. This is a book that tells you that these are morally neutral things that people use to seek lasting happiness – something that these fake rabbits can never produce. Fake rabbits and real rabbits are not mutually exclusive. It's just that the chase of fake rabbits tends to hinder the chase of real rabbits. That is when you have a problem.

Use this analogy to guide your actions. Fake rabbits are like mashed potatoes served at Thanksgiving dinner. Assume it's mid-November. You call your mom

---

81   Dr. David Mashburn, *The Benefits of Being Well Liked*, WORK PUZZLE HOMEPAGE, April 20, 2010, http://tinyurl.com/zvbmvz4.

and tell her that you are so excited to come over for Thanksgiving. You cannot wait for a home cooked meal – especially the mashed potatoes which are always your favorite. Your mom says, "We can't wait to have you home, honey. The whole family is going to be here this year and your little sisters cannot wait to hug you. There is just one piece of bad news. We will not have mashed potatoes this year. We just couldn't get any good ones at the store so we left them off the menu." Would you really then say, "No mashed potatoes! Well, in that case, I am not coming."

Of course not. You would go to Thanksgiving dinner to be around the people important in your life, to catch up, reminisce, and to partake in conversation. You would go for the love of family and to celebrate your blessings. However, if the mashed potatoes somehow show up on the table – you eat them. Mashed potatoes at Thanksgiving dinner is an apt description of how you should think of money, good looks, and popularity. These are side dishes to the real rabbits you need to chase. They won't keep you from dinner (i.e., living the life you desire) but, if these things show up as you focus on what matters, then by all means gobble them up.

Horace Greeley hit the nail on the head when he said, "Fame is a vapor, popularity an accident, and riches take wings. Only one thing endures and that is character." He skipped looks, but I'm sure the idea was implied. Now let's take a brief look at what's worth chasing in your life. These real rabbits are the focus of the rest of the book.

REAL RABBITS

If I am going to tell you what not to chase, then I certainly must tell you what to chase. That's only fair as you must focus your attention somewhere. After thinking about this exact topic for over a decade, I have narrowed the list down to three things a person needs to be happy. The following chapters lay them out in detail, but let me give you an inside peek. The real rabbits in life are:

1. A strong sense of peace and contentment with your life;
2. Serious relationships with a few real friends; and

3. Solid character (the desire to live the life of a moral person)

These desires are universal. It turns out we want the same things because we are all beautifully, equally human in our quest for real happiness and authentic lives. I have found that these real rabbits do not change based on a person's race, religion, sex, disability, sexual orientation, or anything else. The only caveat is that they become more apparent with age. The means we employ to seek these rabbits may differ but the ends remain the same.

For example, a religious person may find contentment and peace in God whereas an atheist may find it in nature or science. The end is the same – peace and contentment. A Utilitarian may believe character is developed when the greatest good possible is done whereas a Deontologist may believe character grows with a focus on moral duties. Again, the end is the same – the desire to live the life of a moral person. Someone may love traveling with a small group of friends while someone else prefers family movie night. The end is the same – the development and cultivation of serious relationships.

Yet, we spend too much time these days breaking up into little groups. We believe that these exclusive associations will bring us closer to our own real rabbits – which must be different from those outside our little group, right? College campuses are a notorious for this practice. Diversity is a buzz word in academia, but then you see the liberal arts students go one way, the business students another. You rarely see the Multicultural Excellence group put on an event in tandem with the Evangelical Ministry group. People seem to love the idea of diversity but only if it occurs within their preferred groups or between groups that would otherwise hang out anyway. Everyone ends up in their corner and students feel pressure to take one side or the other. It's a shame because they then miss vital chances to develop their character as one big learning community.

I am asked all the time how I will change my message for the particular group I am about to address. Event organizers will say something like, "Okay, so you have a room full of [athletes, multicultural students, international students, police officers, engineers, or accountants], how are you going to modify your message?"

I reply that I do not have major changes planned. Of course, I promise not to talk about seeking popularity with a group of engineers or employee morale at

Greek Week. But overall, I tell them that the outcome is always better when my message is the same for everyone.

"But why? They ask. "Don't you want to focus on what MY people chase in THEIR lives?"

This prompt allows me to make a very valuable observation:

The chasing of real rabbits is a radically inclusive endeavor. The desire for contentment, relationships, and character applies to all of us, equally. We don't need to cluster off into different groups for once. Just think about it this way: It's not as if women want contentment in their lives while men do not. It's not as if athletes desire strong friendships while members of the chess club do not. Why would a police officer desire to become an honest person while a doctor would not? Our associations may dovetail with our interests, advance our agendas, or reinforce our heritage, but they do not influence what makes human beings authentically happy. The real rabbits in life are hard wired into people and we all find our mark in the same place. We are all beautifully, equally human when it comes to character.

Isn't that refreshing?

PART II:
GET SET

CHAPTER 8:

CONTENTMENT

"There are billions of people across this Earth who would love to have your worst day."
– Justin Jones-Fosu

"I am content; that is a blessing greater than riches; and he to whom that is given need ask no more."
– Henry Fielding

Contentment is a prerequisite to happiness. This is a fundamental truth of life. You just don't encounter a discontented happy person; that would be an oxymoron like the walking dead or deafening silence. I have yet to encounter a soul who finds this real rabbit is insignificant. No one says, "Contentment. That's not for me. I don't mind spending each day uncomfortable in my own skin, unsure of my beliefs and relationships, and stressed about my future." We all want to wake up at peace with who we are, what we believe, who we love, where we are today, and our plans for the tomorrow. Though the connection to happiness is obvious, this chapter focuses on the nuances and the reasons why people seeking contentment struggle. This conversation might be difficult for Americans, a prosperous yet discontented flock. Being content with one's life is critical to authentic happiness, however, so I am compelled to bring up the topic.

Let's start with a definition: Con·tent·ment (*noun*) = internal satisfaction with who you are now and where you are going, the attainment and maintenance of which does not require fake rabbits or external changes. The best synonyms for contentment are comfort, gratefulness, fulfillment, and peace. You can see why people crave this real rabbit. Who wouldn't love to wake up more fulfilled and comfortable? The concept should be examined in three parts.

First, to be content, your satisfaction must be internalized and made a part of your nature. This means that it must be authentic. Merely appearing content is insufficient even though we excel at faking it from time to time. We don our "I'm happy" face, take some deep breaths, and pretend we are at peace with our existence. At first glance, the world may not catch on. We have all witnessed couples, discontented in some way, take it out on each other. They fight and yell like crazy in private. But when a neighbor walks in they stop and look as content as ever. They can morph into fake-contentment mode so quickly that an outsider might miss the truth. But this persona is superficial and their discomfort stays bundled up internally – the exact opposite of contentment.

Our "I'm happy" face is what society expects and so we provide it, regardless of whether we feel happy. We fake contentment more than we chase contentment. This irony explains why most people, upon first impression, seem content. Then, after a few rendezvous and a bit more trust, we witness the façade break down and dissatisfaction appear. An internal state of discontentment is tough to hide over time; our true colors bleed through. The bottom line is that this real rabbit requires your "I'm happy" face to be authentic. In lieu of faking it all the time, this chapter will help you analyze your life and recognize that an authentic, internal state of contentment is available to you at any time, for free. You must only change your perspective on what's worthy of worry.

Second, contentment does not require any fake rabbits or external changes. Rather, truly content people remain satisfied <u>regardless</u> of whether they get a raise, buy new furniture or clothes, become more attractive, or make the news. These things might make them happy, but their overall happiness does not depend on any these outcomes. Bad things may happen to them and that makes them sad, but their contentment gauge stays consistent. You can choose to be content even during a tough season of your life. Doesn't it sound wonderful to have your contentment level within your control and outside the randomness of external, uncontrollable events?

A prime example of this second point occurs when we look to the future to fill our contentment deficit. Too often we say, "Well, I will be content when this week is over. I'm just so busy now." When that doesn't pan out, we say, "Well, I'll find some peace when this month is over. Things will calm down then and I'll get back on track." When that doesn't pan out either, we extend the timeframe. Now it's a semester or a financial quarter and then it becomes the number of months that remain in the year. This explains why people eagerly anticipate New Year's Eve – a chance to start over. But, as the famous quote states, "Insanity is doing the same thing over and over again and expecting different results."[82] The point is that January 1 is still just January 1 and nothing about a particular date will cure our discontentment unless we adopt a different approach. Truly content people do not have to wait for contentment; this virtue is a consistent part of their being throughout the year.

Third, contentment now does not require sacrifice of your goals and dreams. Your future certainly still matters. It is nonsense when people say things like, "I never want to be content with where I am in life. I always want to be better." They misunderstand the concept. It is silly to think that people do not want to be content today – everyone does. Remember, however, part of being content is an internal satisfaction with your now <u>and</u> your future. That's why this is a real rabbit.

Generally, people who lack goals, dreams, and a desire to improve are rarely content because satisfaction about a future track is part of the contentment package. So, you can be content with your today and still push to be better tomorrow. That's the whole point and much more effective than expending

---

82   This quote is often attributed to Albert Einstein, but some have been unable to trace it to his writings. *See* Michael Becker, *Einstein on Misattribution: "I Probably Didn't Say That,"* BECKER'S ONLINE JOURNAL, November 13, 2012, http://tinyurl.com/lombm5p. Regardless of who said it, this is an amazingly telling quote that we should apply to our lives immediately.

maximum effort in the hope that someday, when you achieve some subset of goals, you will finally find some peace.

Contentment, Where Art Thou?

Just because everyone desires contentment does not make it prevalent. It turns out that a clear majority of Americans are discontented with their lives. Yet they live and breathe in an environment that should provide contentment in abundance. Many Americans entertain three misperceptions that create this disconnect.

THE FIRST MISPERCEPTION: my down days are as bad as anyone's

Many Americans enjoy the luxury of worrying about the more trivial things in life and so we do. We have adapted to our standard of living and now seek a more perfect existence. The idea is compelling – humanity should strive to improve the standard of living. The problem is that nothing we create will ever be perfect. Stuff will still break. Internet connections will sometimes be slow and rush hour will always be infuriating (even if you're in a vehicle that drives itself; be careful). When things bog down instead of becoming faster, sleeker, and cooler, we experience discontentment. Our current possessions get old and no longer create the excitement we imagined. Fewer and fewer purchases produce lasting contentment and we feel like we deserve better. We chase and chase. We misperceive how astonishingly good we live as compared to the rest of the world. We close our eyes to the fact that there are billions of people around the world who would love to have our bad days.

THE SECOND MISPERCEPTION: a full life = a content life

We pack our lives are so full that we leave little space for contentment to take hold and flourish. Finding contentment is like growing a garden. A successful gardener finds a plot, thoroughly prepares the dirt, plants seeds, and waits. It takes time, a good amount of sunlight, proper maintenance, and plenty of space for the seeds to germinate and grow into beautiful flowers. But, if our plot remains full of other stuff throughout this process, the seeds will struggle to grow. This is a metaphor for contemporary America. We are so busy doing and going and buying and wanting that we become disconnected from Socrates' warning to beware of the barrenness of a busy life. This over-programming is exhausting. We misperceive that a bustling life = a content life.

THE THIRD MISPERCEPTION: a successful life by society's standards = a content life

Let's face it, most of us have what we need to be happy. We simply lose track of our prosperity in our full-throttle drive to succeed. Ironically, this misperception has little to do with our quest to become more intelligent, talented, physically fit, or virtuous. An abundance of these things actually adds contentment to a life and should be our focus. Rather, it's our push to be more well-off by society's standards – think richer, more beautiful, more professionally accomplished, more esteemed – that merely moves us around in a circle like Cash chasing pretend rabbits. Often, our hard work pays off because we're smart and driven. Now we have more of everything except contentment, hence the third misperception. Neel Burton nailed it:

If I am to believe everything that I see in the media, happiness is to be six foot tall or more and to have bleached teeth and a firm abdomen, all the latest clothes, accessories, and electronics, a picture-perfect partner of the opposite sex who is both a great lover and a terrific friend, an assortment of healthy and happy children, a pet that is neither a stray nor a mongrel, a large house in the right sort of neighborhood, a second property in an idyllic holiday location, a top-of-the-range car to shuttle back and forth from the one to the other, a clique of 'friends' with whom to have fabulous dinner parties, three or four foreign holidays a year, and a high-impact job that does not distract from any of the above.[83]

---

83 Neel Burton, MD, *Why Success Won't Make You Happy: A Critique of Conventional Success*, PSYCHOLOGY TODAY, November 21, 2013, http://tinyurl.com/z5tbonp.

And, of course, the attainment of all this is impossible. This makes a lot of us chase harder and faster towards a goal that always outpaces us. Others give up unsatisfied.

This chapter will shine a light on these misperceptions in turn by taking you on adventures to three beautiful places – rural Peru, Paris, and a quaint Mexican fishing village. These trips are meant to demonstrate the irony in the typical American struggle to find contentment in a place where people generally have everything they need to be happy. I am grateful to have you along for the ride. You may take the window seat and imagine a beautiful life full of contentment.

MISPERCEPTION ONE: THE IRONIC AMERICAN STRUGGLE WITH CONTENTMENT

Americans struggle to find a strong and lasting sense of contentment. At least that is what they admit when asked in anonymous surveys. People have little to lose by lying in such a forum, so I put some stock in these numbers. Especially when every survey I encounter draws the same conclusions. I was baffled by the results of just such a poll from a few years ago. It was designed to measure the percentage of Americans who possess exactly the type of contentment I am interested in – the authentic kind. The poll was anonymous and there was just one question:

In the morning, do you <u>consistently</u> and <u>genuinely</u> wake up happy?

This question touches all the right bases when it comes to contentment. Notice the question does not ask whether you wake up tired? Most of us are a little slow on the uptake early in the morning. The question also does not ask whether you ever have a bad day, week, month, year. We all do – life is tough and unpredictable. Murphy's Law that whatever can go wrong, will go wrong seems to follow us like a little black cloud sometimes. Instead, the question is very specific. It asks whether you consistently – <u>over time</u> – and genuinely – <u>authentically</u> – wake up happy. It is written perfectly to probe the depth of our contentment. Before we move on, please take a minute or two to close your eyes and honestly answer that same question.

Now make sure you are sitting down because the results may startle you. A whopping 67% of Americans answered, "No." They admitted that they don't consistently and genuinely wake up happy with their lives … in this country! Similar surveys reinforce this point. A 2016 Harris poll, called the Happiness Index found that two out of every three Americans are not all that happy with their lives. [84]These results mirror polls from years past.[85] It turns out that men are less content than women and that our younger generations have the lowest levels of contentment – a mere 28% to 31% of our 18 to 38 year-olds respond as happy.[86] The numbers also show that the contentment of Americans is not increasing even as our economy grows and standard of living advances.[87] This demonstrates yet again that a person's joy, affection, and tranquility are not tied to economic enrichment.

This is America, People!

These statistics are shocking and depressing at the same time. Before I saw the results, I thought the percentage of discontented Americans would be much lower. But, after seeing the actual percentages time and again, I thought about the people I encounter every day. I would venture that around 30% of the people I work with seem authentically content on a consistent basis. The other 70%, not so much. Perhaps I just don't know them, but many seem downright miserable. How about your colleagues?

Let's move outside of the office. I don't see a ton of happy and content people on my commute. Do you? What about running errands or out on the town? Do you see many content-looking people when you are out to dinner, on an airplane, or even out jogging? I cannot say that I do.

---

84 *Latest Happiness Index Reveals American Happiness at All-Time Low*, THE HARRIS POLL, July 8, 2016, http://tinyurl.com/hpa3wtj. In this poll, only 31% of Americans identified as "very happy" with their lives.

85 Carolyn Gregoire, *Happiness Index: Only 1 In 3 Americans Are Very Happy*, According to Harris Poll, HUFFINGTON POST, June 5, 2013, http://tinyurl.com/kddr6l2.

86 Ibid.

87 *Are You Happy? It May Depend on Age, Race/Ethnicity and Other Factors: Happiness on the Decline for Several American Population Subsets* - Minorities, Recent Grads and Disabled, THE HARRIS POLL, May 30, 2013, http://tinyurl.com/jg8kynk.

Try this experiment next time you are out and about. Smile at ten people as you walk. Don't do it all creepy or you'll ruin my experiment. Just use a gentle, "I'm a friendly human," type smile. I have done this hundreds of times and found that only about three in ten people smile back at me; most act like even having to acknowledge my existence or look away from their phone is a burden. I don't interfere in their lives any more deeply than a smile and a nod and even that makes many people grimace. That's the amazing thing about anonymous polls, I guess – outside of politics, they usually get stuff like this right. And that makes me upset for one main reason … this is America, people!

Creating an environment where people could live in freedom and peace has been the goal of this country since our Declaration of Independence. The founders used the words "life, liberty and the pursuit of happiness," – the equivalent of "the good life" in the 1700s. Our system of government was purposely structured toward this end. America is unique in that it has functioned as an (imperfect) representative democracy since its founding – a political structure that was beyond a radical idea at the time. While the United States is not the first nation to include elements of democracy, "it is the oldest existing nation with a constitutional government in which the people elect their own government and representatives."[88]

To this end, today we spend billions on national defense and police forces so our people can work, rest, raise families, and improve society without fear. There is very little that we owe our government in exchange – we are only required to obey the law, pay taxes, serve on juries (and show up to court if summoned), register for the draft (just the men for now), and buy health insurance. These are our only mandatory civic duties.

Most nations struggle to provide the level of freedom enjoyed by Americans. The United States strives to, and for the most part does, supply key human services such as power, water, trash collection, and medical care to even our most rural locations. Our justice system is imperfect, but as fair as it gets in the world. Ask yourself whether you would rather face a criminal trial in another country? Air travel is a pain, but we have little doubt that we will arrive at our destinations

88 Sarah Hauer, *Paul Ryan Claims the US is the 'Oldest Democracy' in the World. Is He Right?* POLTI FACT, July 11, 2016, http://tinyurl.com/jtpjlqw. The article rated Paul Ryan's claim that the United States is "the oldest democracy in the world" as "True."

safely and on time. There are no armed checkpoints on our highways. Most our neighborhoods are very safe. Our charitable giving ranks second in the world in terms of giving money, helping strangers, and volunteering time.[89] It turns out that 61% of Americans do such good works consistently.[90]

Make no mistake about it, our system is far from perfect. Pick up a newspaper or ask around and that fact becomes clear. America is still rife with corruption, unfairness, and inequality. We have race relations issues that must be addressed. Our public schools need a major boost and our teachers should be paid better. No one should feel left out of the American dream and some clearly do. But, the foundation for contentment that this nation provides today is as strong and stable as exists in the world. At least we can argue about the country's problems and criticize our government in peace and without fear while surfing the Internet on our new iPads and sipping a latte in a swanky Starbucks.

The bottom line is that, in America, we are free to seek our dreams. In America, we can grow up with little and gain much. We make our own lives here. In America, a poor kid whose parents did not earn college degrees can grow up and become a law professor at a prestigious university. This lawyer can then marry another poor kid from a broken home who worked hard and became a surgeon. Those success stories just do not happen nearly as often in many other places. If you are born poor in other countries, you stay poor. If you are born into an uneducated family, you stay uneducated. Therefore, if people truly want to seek contentment, they should be able to find it in abundance in America. So, the fact that two thirds of Americans wake up unhappy is shocking to say the least. It could be much worse.

MACHU PICCHU, RURAL PERU & THE CONTENTMENT AT YOUR FINGERTIPS

Let me add some perspective to these disturbing contentment percentages. My wife and I traveled to Machu Picchu. Peru is stunning and we highly

---

89 *See* Quentin Fottrell, *America is the (Second) Most Generous Country in the World,* MARKET WATCH, November 12, 2015, http://tinyurl.com/zjqxumo. We ranked behind Myanmar of all places – a country where 66% of the population engages in charitable giving.
90 Ibid.

recommend you visit this "Wonder of the World" (there are only seven on the list). Make sure to take this trip when you're younger. To get to Machu Picchu, you first fly to Lima – Peru's capital city. Then you fly to Cuzco – the historic capital of the Inca Empire. Then, you hop on a train for a three-and-a-half-hour ride to Aguas Calientes. This is a picturesque little village located at the bottom of a gorge at the foot of the ancient ruins. There are no roads into Aguas Calientes – you either hike or take the train. Now that is remote! Then, you jump on a bus for a half-hour roller coaster ride to Machu Picchu. Finally, you walk uphill the rest of the way. It drains you, but the journey is worth it in so many ways.

The most fascinating part of getting to Machu Picchu is that you get to see rural Peru. There is a unique, positive spirit to the Peruvian people. They know they live in a magical place. But, the stunning beauty of the scenery is in brutal contrast with the nation's deep poverty. Life is particularly tough in rural Peru where the poverty rate hovers around 54% while the economy blossoms in the urban areas.[91] These poverty issues have roots in: "high rates of illiteracy, particularly among women, lack of essential services, such as education and electrical power, insecure rights to land, forests and water … and poor transportation infrastructure and marketing systems."[92]

We deal with these issues in the United States to be sure, but not nearly to this degree. There is too much poverty here (nearly 15% of Americans at last count),[93] but our rate is seven percentage points less than Peru's national poverty rate and more than three times lower than Peru's rural poverty rate.[94] The poverty line in America is $11,700 in annual income per person.[95] In Peru, it is mere dollars per day or just

---

91   Maria Arana, *Peru's Poor*, NEW YORK TIMES: OP-ED PAGE, march 20, 2013, http://tinyurl.com/hrnx7r2. See also, Monica Roth, *Contrasting Poverty in Lima and the Countryside*, BORGEN MAGAZINE, September 3, 2014, http://tinyurl.com/hoajpw8.

92   *Rural Poverty in Peru*, RURAL POVERTY PORTAL, http://tinyurl.com/m4fq485, (last visited August 27, 2016).

93   See Carmen DeNavas-Walt and Bernadette D. Proctor, *Income and Poverty in the United States: 2014: Current Population Reports*, UNITED STATES CENSUS BUREAU, September 2015, http://tinyurl.com/oskydlu. The most up to date data is from 2014.

94   *See Juan Moreno Belmar, Enabling Poor Rural People to Overcome Poverty in Peru*, INTERNATIONAL FUND FOR AGRICULTURAL DEVELOPMENT, July 2013, http://tinyurl.com/gmrz4b9.

95   *Federal Poverty Level Guidelines*, OBAMACARE FACTS, http://obamacarefacts.com/federal-poverty-level/. The most up to date data is from 2016.

over $100 a month.[96] Our educational system struggles in many ways, but schools in rural Peru face a more dire reality with rural Peruvian students falling well below the worldwide average in reading, science, and math. [97] And, that's just in places where schools exist at all.[98] Our power goes out from time to time, but electricity in rural Peru is a blessing as one third of the country lives without access to the nation's electrical grid.[99] Nearly eight million people in Peru do not have access to piped water.[100] We lament public transportation in America, but the infrastructure in rural Peru is in desperate need of improvement. Data shows that "eight in nine rural Peruvians lack access to basic infrastructure – such as electricity, clean water, and good roads – that could help them climb out of poverty."[101] The reality is that if Peru were your home versus the United States, then you would:

- Die 6.33 years sooner and be 3.3 times more likely to die in infancy
- Be 50% more likely to be unemployed
- Make 78.98% less money
- Spend 96.21% less money on health care
- Use 90.68% less electricity
- Be 76.32% more likely to be murdered
- Experience 6.89% more of a class divide[102]

96   Manuel Vigo, *Decrease in Peruvians living below poverty line*, PERU THIS WEEK, May 8, 2013, http://tinyurl.com/z7yeh5d.
97   Milagros Salazar, PERU: *Rural Education Reflects Ethnic, Socioeconomic Inequalities*, INTER PRESS SERVICE NEWS AGENCY, January 31, 2011, http://tinyurl.com/zx49hbg. *See also Peru: Student Performance* (PISA 2012), ORGANIZATION FOR ECONOMIC COOPERATION AND DEVELOPMENT, August 27, 2016, http://tinyurl.com/jmpo5rd.
98   There are 44,480 educational institutions in rural areas of Peru, including 22,000 primary schools. In one-fourth of the cases, the students' homes are far from their schools. Many students live with other families during the week to attend school, returning to their rural homes only on weekends or during school breaks. In 2006, only 13 percent of rural villages and towns had secondary schools." Ibid.
99   Katherine Tweed, *Peru Will Provide Solar Power to Half a Million Poor Households*, IEEE SPECTRUM, July 30, 2013, http://tinyurl.com/z4vrfnl.
100 Angel Paez, *Clean Water Costing A Fortune For Peru's Poor*, THE HUFFINGTON POST, May 25, 2011, http://tinyurl.com/d6xxzk.
101 *Bringing Basic Infrastructure to Rural Peru*, GRUPO DE ANÁLISIS PARA EL DESARROLLO (GRADE), August 27, 2016, http://tinyurl.com/jrbpm9m.
102 *Compare the US to Peru*, IF IT WERE MY HOME, August 27, 2016, http://tinyurl.com/hmwv3q4.

Despite these serious quality of life issues, the main thing that stood out was that rural Peruvians still seemed content. We noticed this attitude in the shops, at meals, and just walking the streets. People opened doors and gave up their seats on the train. They gave us directions even though our Spanish was dreadful. Meals were cooked with pride and people looked out for each other. This perception is common for people who visit rural Peru. One visitor described the same vibe more vividly:

Although the poverty in Peru was evident in many of the towns that I visited, also evident was the spirit of the Peruvian people. At no time during my trip did it seem that individuals in the towns were unhappy with their situation. Children played soccer, elders sat on the porches and watched the world go by, and those giving my friend and me tours for reasonable sums were passionate about the landscapes of their country. This was perhaps the most inspiring for me, for even without wealth the people of Peru are able to live fulfilling lives and be generous and welcoming to those around them, even foreigners. It is these kinds of people that are worthy of help, and it is important to remember that people in poverty are not much different from you and me.[103]

You are likely aware by now that none of this is meant to throw stones at Peru. My intent is the exact opposite. I am confused and frustrated as to what's happening in America! Let me put this a different way. All I could think about heading back to the Lima Airport was, "Wait, a second. The rural Peruvians have it far worse in terms of basic human needs, essential services, and amenities and yet seven out of every ten AMERICANS don't wake up happy!"

In the United States, we joke about first world problems like slow Internet connections, poor cell phone reception, and having to wait in fifteen-minute

103 Katherine Pickle, *5 things I Learned about Poverty in Peru*, THE BORGEN PROJECT, June 28, 2015, http://tinyurl.com/hgtbg77.

security lines at the airport. But the reality is we take these minor inconveniences so seriously that they actually keep us from finding much peace. Combine that with our "Keeping Up with the Joneses" mentality and you have the American recipe for discontentment. We are a people of, "I want more until whatever I get wears out or slows down and then I want something better, faster, and sleeker." Americans face the same dilemma posed by Socrates centuries ago when he wrote, "He who is not contented with what he has, would not be contented with what he would like to have."

The upshot of all this resides in the quote leading off this chapter – "There are billions of people across this Earth who would love to have your worst day." Let's put ideology aside and face the facts. We can debate American exceptionalism all day long. I do believe that this country is exceptional, but that is not my focus here. My point rests on something prior to that debate and much more fundamental. The United States, warts and all, provides the best foundation in the world to chase after contentment. It is a nation specifically designed for people to achieve their dreams, find peace, and improve their standard of living. Of course, like anyone else, Americans still wake up tired and go through stretches of discontentment when bad things happen. That's the price everyone pays in life. But over time, if a person cannot find a strong sense of contentment here … the chances are good that they are chasing something fake.

MISPERCEPTION TWO: "BEWARE THE BARRENNESS OF A BUSY LIFE." – SOCRATES

Imagine a young couple visiting France. Upon arriving in Paris, they are urged to follow the crowds to look at art and other beautiful things. The Louvre, the Orsay Museum, the Museum of Modern Art, Notre Dame, the Arc de Triomphe, the Eiffel Tower are all located in that city for crying out loud. Imagine that this couple isn't into museum hopping. They certainly are not art experts and would rather relax on a Seine river cruise. However, they are in Paris and feel compelled to take in some art. So, they head to the Louvre – the world's largest museum housed in a centuries-old palace of the French kings. They wait in line forever, walk in, and find the place is packed.[104] They see the Mona Lisa and the Venus de Milo and then exit to find a quieter museum. The Orsay Museum is down the road a bit, but it's jammed full too. Finally, they decide to try the Musée de l'Orangerie – a building designed to shelter orange trees through the winter and located in the King's garden. It is much smaller and houses some famous paintings including Monet's *Water Lilies*. As they walk through the door, signs greet them prohibiting much of what they had been doing all day: "No flash photography. Check your bags and snacks at the door. No cellphones. Observe silence." Security at the entrance is tight and guards hover everywhere watching people closely. Rules are strictly enforced.

The couple moves to the Monet wing and the art is stunning. It's Impressionism - meaning that you must to look at the painting for a few seconds before you realize that you are seeing a person, a landscape, a flower, all in simulated motion. They head to a corner of the museum and see a traveling art exhibit. It is not a Monet for sure and it is hideous. It looks like every color imaginable has been tossed onto the canvas with an ice cream scoop held by someone wearing a blindfold. Just looking at it gives them a headache. If this was Impressionism, they were not impressed.

But, they were in Paris. Tourists are not critical of the art in Paris. To their eyes, everything is a masterpiece. To that end, people gather around this work, put their fingers to their chins, and utter profundities like, "Wow. This is a stunningly-beautiful representation of the post-modern world." And "It's so lovely. It has such depth." The husband couldn't stand it any longer.

He looks at his wife and bellows, "Are you kidding me? That painting sucks. It's the ugliest piece of art I've ever seen." Others look over while his wife laughs in nervous agreement.

The guards notice them making fun of this apparently-important work of art. They approach the couple with a perturbed look on a grizzled face.

---

104 Almost 9 million people visit the Louvre each year – that's over 30,000 a day. *See* Max Kutner, *Louvre to Reopen After Historic Paris Floods*, NEWSWEEK, June 6, 2016, http://tinyurl.com/hnma7l3 (stating More than 9 million people visited the Louvre in 2014 . . . which the French government has said makes it the most visited museum in the world. As of 2014, the museum had 446,673 works in its inventory.").

The wife kicks her husband subtly in the leg and says, "Here they come. How's your French? What are you going to say when the guards get over here?"

One perturbed guard nears them and says, in broken English, "I see that you are laughing at our new piece of art. Do you know who painted that? Do you know how much that picture is worth?

The wife subtly kicks her husband again and whispers, "Just lie. Tell him you love it."

The husband decides to be honest. He replies, "I don't like it. I think it sucks. Just looking at it gives me a headache."

Bang! His wife kicks him harder at this point. All subtly is gone.

The guard exclaims, growing ever more frustrated, "Excuse me. Did you say it sucks? No one has ever said that to me before."

The wife chimes in, "I wonder why!" This is turning ugly fast.

Unexpectedly, the guard's countenance softens, "Since you said that, I am going to tell you a secret. You should know something about this painting. It's supposed to "suck" as you say. That was the artist's intention. He wasn't trying to paint something beautiful. Instead, he used every color imaginable and painted them all haphazardly onto the canvas."

The husband retorts, "I was right? I mean, there was no ice cream scoop or blindfold involved. But, that was a pretty good guess for a non-art guy."

The guard continues, "The painting is supposed to give you a headache. The artist is trying to depict the barrenness on an overly busy life."

Just ponder that wisdom for a second. The bareness of an overly busy life! The couple just stands there, stunned by those words, until the husband mutters, "Well, no wonder it's giving me a headache. That's my life!"

And they left. It was on to a different landmark. But now they were pondering the pictures they painted in their own lives. That intentionally ugly piece of art had an amazing way of shining a light on what they, and people more generally, chase in life.

LET'S PAINT A PICTURE OF YOUR LIFE

Let's evaluate the "full life = a content life" misperception via a forceful thought experiment. Assume that I am: (1) invisible and (2) a capable artist.

These are two things that will never be true, but just work with me here. There's a method to my madness. Assume that you are you without any magical powers. Assume further that I have been commissioned to paint a picture of your life. My instructions require me to depict what defines you and how you spend your time. Assume finally that I must do so accurately and that little artistic license is allowed. I have one month to compete the task. Here's the kicker – the only inputs I can use are:

- The way you act when no one is looking
- The way you treat people who cannot do anything to you or for you
- The way you treat your parents
- The way you treat your kids
- The way you treat your friends
- The words you speak (especially in anger or in stressful situations)
- The virtues or vices upon which you act

That's it. Since actions speak louder than words, my masterpiece will be based solely on what you do as opposed to what you think you ought to do. Keep in mind that I am invisible so you will not have any incentive to act better than you want to. You won't even know I'm there. I also have a month, so your bad days will be averaged with your best days. This means that your painting will be as accurate as possible. Under these guidelines, would I be able to paint a picture you desire? Would you be proud to display it? Or, would I be forced to take all the colors on my palette and just splatter all over the canvas muttering, "I have no idea what this person stands for?"

We each want to paint a positive picture of who we are and what we value. The problem is the rest of the stuff in our life interferes. Our lives often feel barren even though our to-do list never ends. We hustle and bustle about and still feel lonely. Let this story be a catalyst for you. If you seek a sense of contentment and peace in your life, then something must give. Like any garden, you have to clear out space so the seeds you plant have room to grow. A later chapter on Priorities will explain how to do this in detail. For now, be thinking about what should stay and what needs to go. Let's lose the misperception that a full and busy life is a better life.

MISPERCEPTION THREE: A SUCCESSFUL LIFE = A CONTENT LIFE

Contentment also remains elusive due to our push for worldly success. Most of us are always looking for a better job, a higher salary, more respect, nicer stuff, and a larger nest egg. Basically, we push to build our careers, finances, possessions, reputations, and retirement savings – our WORLDLY PORTFOLIO. We want this portfolio to bulge in the future so we push as hard as we can in the present. Problematically, these efforts often come at the expense of contentment-building assets such as our character, family, friends, hobbies, and talents – our REAL RABBITS PORTFOLIO. There just is not time to tend to both sets of priorities. This divide swells as we age. The fear of limited time left to contribute rears its head and we feel we must choose. Amidst the chaos, it is easy to forget that we may already have all we need to be happy. We willingly enter a race designed to build a WORLDLY PORTFOLIO that disconnects us from our goal.

THE RACE OF YOUR LIFE

Picture a massive group of runners near the starting line of a marathon. But, this is no ordinary marathon – the course has been extended indefinitely and no official route has been posted. But the runners don't know this. They hope to recognize markers from time to time that point the way. Their goal is to reach the finish line as quickly as possible. The finish line is where the good stuff is. This is where they can finally find some peace. The finish line is where they can spend more time with their families and friends. Once the race is over, they will have virtually unlimited time for hobbies and travel. Their journey, however, will be arduous and exhausting.

None of them have a reason to run this fast or so far – there isn't an official timer and nothing will happen if they proceed much slower or veer off onto a different path. For some, this is more of an ego thing. They are desperate to compete, to outrun others in the race. For others, this is a race they feel society expects them to run. This is just what you do if you want to live the good life. Most all of them labor under the misperception that a successful life = a content life.

Picture everyone's families and friends standing right with their runners at the starting line, cheering them on. These people have helped prepare these runners for the race of their life. Some are hesitant about the whole thing, but they want their loved ones to be happy and achieve their goals and dreams.

The runners take their marks and the gun sounds; they're off! They run fast at first. Time passes and some slow down while others keep charging forward. More time passes and some break down and must stop. Others slow to a crawl, but few turn back. The finish line is somewhere in the distance – they can sense it. Many lament the time spent away from their loved ones. Others lament the fact that their sole focus is on this race. But they follow the leaders and race on. More time passes and passes and, eventually, they enter the home stretch. As they reach the finish line, they are exhausted. They embrace their families and friends … who haven't moved an inch! It turns out that the starting line and finish line of this race were in the same place. The marathon was a big circle right back to their loved ones and support systems.

The runners received some benefits from the race to be sure. They are in better shape and have accumulated a lot of the benefits tied to hard work. Some can even brag about their finishing position. But, most find it difficult to enjoy the fruits of their labor once they realize that they stand exhausted at the exact same place they started. Their loved ones were there all along and now these runners are desperate to make up for lost time. They pray that these relationships haven't frayed too drastically from the neglect.

The moral of the story couldn't be more clear – beware of chasing fake rabbits to achieve the life you may already have. By all means, strive to improve your standard of living. It is wonderful not to have to worry about paying the bills. By all means, spend the time and energy it takes become a better version of yourself. It is important to leave a professional legacy. Please improve your talents and make an impact in this world. But, just make sure to pace yourself and seek these things with a sense of balance. Honor your priorities. Don't ignore the people standing right by you in an effort to come back to them with more worldly things to offer. They don't want that; they want you.

Now we see the third misperception in action. We believe in success, so much so that we dedicate our best energy and attention to its achievement. And, our race is never over because there is no finish line, unless we die trying, and no one ever tells us to stop running. But, we run on in the belief that the pleasure of the finish will be greater than the pain of the race. However, that really just depends on where you are standing.

THE FABLE OF THE MEXICAN FISHERMAN

Finding contentment without falling prey to the seductiveness of the rat race reminds me of a classic fable about an American executive and a Mexican fisherman. The story is so good I reproduce it in full to end this chapter on contentment. The story speaks for itself and will put this entire chapter in proper perspective. Enjoy!

An American executive was taking a much-needed vacation in a Mexican coastal village when a small boat with just one fisherman docked. Inside the small boat were several large yellow fin tuna. The American complimented the Mexican fisherman on the quality of his fish and asked how long it took him to catch them.

"Not very long," answered the Mexican.

"But then, why didn't you stay out longer and catch more?" asked the American.

The Mexican explained that his small catch was sufficient to meet his needs and those of his family.

The American asked, "But what do you do with the rest of your time?"

"I sleep late, fish a little, play with my children, and take a siesta with my wife. In the evenings, I go into the village to see my friends, have a few drinks, play the guitar, and sing a few songs... I have a busy and full life."

The American interrupted, "I have an MBA from Harvard and I can help you! You should start by fishing longer every day. You can then sell the extra fish you catch. With the extra revenue, you can buy a bigger boat."

"And after that?" asked the Mexican.

"With the extra money the larger boat will bring, you can buy a second one and a third one and so on until you have an entire fleet of trawlers. Instead of selling your fish to a middle man, you can then negotiate directly with the processing plants and maybe even open your own plant. You can then leave this little village and move to Mexico City, Los Angeles, or even New York City! From there you can direct your huge new enterprise."

"How long would that take?" asked the Mexican.

"Twenty, perhaps 25 years," replied the American.

"And after that?" the Mexican asked.

"Afterwards? That's when it gets really interesting," answered the American, laughing. "When your business gets really big, you can start selling stocks and make millions!"

"Millions? Really? And after that?"

"After that you'll be able to retire, live in a tiny village near the coast, sleep late, play with your children, catch a few fish, take a siesta with your wife and spend your evenings drinking and enjoying your friends."[105]

---

105 This fable is adapted from *Anekdote zur Senkung der Arbeitsmoral, (Anecdote Concerning the Lowering of Productivity)* and is a short story from the German author Heinrich Böll. This is considered one of his best stories for its profound wisdom.

CHAPTER 9:

RELATIONSHIPS

"If you want to go fast, go alone.
But if you want to go far, go together."
— African Proverb

"Truly great friends are hard to find, difficult to leave,
and impossible to forget."
— G. Randolf

"I cannot even imagine where I would be today were it not for that
handful of friends who have given me a heart full of joy.
Let's face it, friends make life a lot more fun."
— Charles R. Swindoll

To become authentically happy, you only need a few <u>real</u> friends. These are people who rush into your life when others rush out.[106] To maintain your integrity, you need a few <u>good</u> friends. These are people who actively seek to

---

106 This is akin to a quote by Walter Winchell that states, "A real friend is one who walks in when the rest of the world walks out."

improve their character. So, what you literally need are a few "really good" (or authentic) friends. But, authentic friends, as I describe them, are hard to find and even harder to keep. As difficult as these friendships may be to develop, this chapter demonstrates why this real rabbit is critically important.

On stage, I address relationships halfway through my speech. I encourage everyone to find some authentic friends. Predictably, the audience nods approvingly, which gives away their thoughts, "That's great, Corey. I've got this. I have a ton of awesome friends." My student audiences take this one step further and think, "That's great, Corey. I've got this. I have a ton of awesome friends. Look at me ... I'm always surrounded by people." This is the moment where minds wander. Most everyone thinks they have their relationships locked down. But I need to be thorough. I must get their attention back. So, next, I say, "You say you are surrounded by people and that is absolutely true. But...have you ever been surrounded by people and friendless?"

Wait, what? Now, everyone is listening again. I tell them that I've certainly felt surrounded yet friendless. In fact, I have been fortunate enough to be surrounded by tons of people at home, at school, and at work since I was little – family, middle school, high school, college, grad school, my tennis students, my employees, and now my college students. I have not led the kind of existence that provides much solitude. Throughout my life, however, I have learned that being surrounded like this is not nearly enough. I have seen my friendships evaporate when I needed them the most. I too have been guilty of bailing when my friends found themselves in need. This taught me that friendship is not about who you have known the longest. Instead, friendship is all about, "who walked into your life and said, I'm here for you and then proved it."[107]

It hurts terribly when you think that people will be there for you and then learn otherwise. Plus, this abandonment always seems to happen during our roughest patches. There are few things harder than being betrayed by a friend. Fortunately, there tends to be a reliable explanation lurking behind the scenes. It revolves around this quote: "We don't lose friends; we just find out who are real ones are."[108] Most of this is preventable. Let me explain.

---

107 The author is unknown.
108 The author is unknown.

WHY FRIENDSHIPS FADE

Most of us experience a gut-wrenching friendship breakup at some point. Others have this experience more regularly. This tends to happen because these friendships weren't authentic to start with. Or, they might have started well, but faded from lack of cultivation. This is usually our own fault. We fail to put in the time, attention, and connection required to find and develop deep friendships. Sometimes it is our friends who do not make the effort. And sometimes, though much more rarely, people just change and drift apart. So, we start over with someone else and cross our fingers. We hope our new friendships will be better and last longer. This is our relationship cycle – we find ourselves surrounded, friendships come, friendships go, we find new friends, and repeat.

THE REAL RABBITS GUIDE TO AUTHENTIC FRIENDSHIPS

The rest of this chapter discusses friendships with a focus on cultivating a few authentic ones. Every situation is different, so these are just guidelines. None of this is meant to identify what is happening in any of your friendships. But, some truth will probably illuminate your situation as these guidelines deal with the most common scenarios. They are true and time-tested. Here are five key takeaways:

1. The Surrounded, Yet Friendless Phenomenon: we are often surrounded by people and are thereby lulled into thinking we have a lot of friends. We hang out, possess common interests, and have fun with these people. Our common environment (school, work) keeps us in close proximity.

2. Then ... we fail to spend the quality time required to nurture these relationships – we are busy, they are busy, and there are just too many people involved. Tough times inevitably happen in our lives and many of these "friends" scatter to the winds. Some betray us, some walk away, and some relationships slowly evaporate. Sometimes we are the cause of the disintegration. We get depressed and then surround ourselves again. The game becomes: find new friends and repeat.

3. Instead ... we must find a select few (three to five) authentic friends and stop. These are people who will rush in to our lives when others rush out. Stopping at a handful gives us the bandwidth to nurture those friendships with significant portions of our time, undivided attention, and emotion. This is hard! But it's doable with three to five people.

4. Nurturing friendships in this way is part of a social contract we make with our friends. We promise to plug in to the relationship and they do too. There is no contract or handshake – these promises are there and they are strong, but they remain implied in all authentic friendships.

5. As we seek and maintain these friendships, we cannot demand that our friends be perfect, because we are not perfect. But we must demand that the people around us be good, because we seek to be good. This principle will help us identify when to move on from a friendship.

Takeaways #1 and #2: Bridesmaids to . . .

Let me tell you a story that explains the surrounded, yet friendless phenomenon. A few years ago, I was asked to be the academic mentor for a sorority. A few of their leaders approached me in tears. Their chapter was in disarray. Grades were low and friendships were splintering for petty reasons. Their reality did not mirror the vision they were sold during recruitment.

These leaders wanted the members to bump up their academics and develop stronger friendships. I wanted to help and so I volunteered. It was an up and down adventure as we struggled to raise GPAs and change the culture. As faculty advisor, I required each member to come meet with me for fifteen minutes each academic term. They would come by with their resumes and we would talk about the organization and the future. Inevitably, they would bring up their friendships. It was a mixed bag – some were content with their relationships and others were more melancholy.

After a few years of similar conversations, I noticed a trend. There was a temporal aspect to the strength of these friendships. The freshman would come to my office time after time in little groups. They were all smiles and would say things like, "Look Professor C, I want you to meet my new friends from my chapter. These are my future bridesmaids." Those statements surprised me at first – how could they know that these would be their best friends for life, especially so soon? But, as I analyzed the comment less analytically, I warmed to the idea. To me, that was the entire point of Greek life. To join a group where you can find some best friends to laugh with and lean on throughout college. The idea is for these friendships to last. Who knows, maybe these people would merit a spot in a future wedding. I would smile and congratulate them on their budding relationships.

But, by senior year, most would come to my office alone. Their smiles were less frequent and they looked more serious about life. I would ask about their friends from first year and their response was shocking. "Oh yeah, those girls. What a bunch of b**ches! We don't even talk anymore. Bridesmaids. I don't think so." I would sympathize with them on these faded friendships. Those conversations shine a light on some pretty hard truths about friendships. I wanted to figure out exactly how this 180-degree turn happened.

So, why the transformation? How could a group of friends this close come to dislike each other so strongly a mere three years later? You know what happened. These people chose to affiliate with a group of people with similar interests. They came in with great enthusiasm. They paid their dues, literally and figuratively, went to the same events and parties, took the same classes, and wore the same color t-shirts (you know who you are). This created the perfect environment to build a friendship – common interests, engaging interaction, fun times, and a group of fellow travelers facing the same hopes and fears. And then life happened. They all got busy. They picked different majors and moved off campus. They got work-study positions and splintered off into other campus organizations they found more intriguing. They remained in the same sorority, but they were members in name only. Little time was available and, therefore, little was allocated to nurturing the friendships. It is as if they thought these tight relationships would last forever merely because of the common affiliation. At least that is the line they were sold upon recruitment. The conclusion is simple: just because you choose to affiliate with a group of people does not make you friends. It takes a good deal of blood (the ability to navigate tough times and stay friends), sweat (the dedication of quality time), and tears (your emotional availability and involvement) that to nurture authentic friendships.

In academia, this problem is not unique to Greek life. I have seen it in student governments, athletic teams, religious associations, and even study groups. It also happens quite frequently in the real world where office cliques, fantasy football leagues, and even book club friendships disintegrate from lack of time and effort. With this principle in mind, it is time to differentiate authentic friendships from the rest.

TAKEAWAY #3: THE SELECT FEW

Everybody needs people who rush into their lives when everyone else rushes out. When you are at your worst, authentic friends stand by your side. These are the people whose mere presence makes your life better and happier. It pains you to let them down and they make you a better person. These are the actual people you would pick to be bridesmaids and groomsmen. But, these types of relationships need nurturing.

If you want people to stay in that category, you need to narrow your friend group down to the select few. Please keep in mind that you only have time for three to five authentic friends. Friendships need our time and uninterrupted attention. This requires that we step away from our phones and plug into these people. Humans crave person-to-person interaction regardless of what generation they were born. As mentioned above, friendships require blood, sweat, and tears. Friendships require loving on people and listening to their problems. Friendships take time and we just do not have enough time for more than a handful. So, please ignore the message from popular culture, implanted since high school, that you need to have a ton of friends to be happy. Those two concepts – (1) many friends and (2) authentic friends - mesh poorly together. To me, you will either have a ton of friends or a few real ones.

Another part of being an authentic friend is the ability to hold each other accountable. In fact, I think accountability is a requirement for any lasting, quality friendship. If you have a friend who is currently struggling in life (think drugs, alcohol, relationships, jobs, cheating, stress, etc.) and you say nothing, you are aiding and abetting that person's demise. Do you think it is appropriate to stand by someone's side while they injure themselves so that you can honor the ideal of never judging a friend? That is nonsense.

This non-judgmental friend is like the person who holds her friend's hair every weekend while she throws up in the toilet from being too drunk at some bar. They cherish this memory because they were "there for each other." I hear this one from my students all the time. Or, the non-judgmental friend who is always the designated driver to make sure his drunk friends get home safely every weekend. People who tell me these stories seem honored to have played this role. They took one for the team again.

I look at the stories completely differently for two reasons. First, every time you take on the role of hair-holder or designated-driver, you are being used as a mere means to an end. Neither of those roles are what you would choose to do with your free time, I hope. These roles are forced on you because of your friends' desires and their expectation that you be loyal. These friendships tend to tilt dangerously out of balance. What your friends expect is excessive loyalty and that is something that you are under no moral obligation to provide. Second, this type of behavior often indicates a much deeper issue with your friends. Negative behavior this intense is often a cry for help or a sign of psychological issues. Standing by someone's side in these cases solely because you don't want to judge them and potentially ruin the friendship is just plain wrong. Authentic friendships can always survive accountability.

The problem lies in how we judge and hold people accountable. We must do these things out of love and compassion instead of contempt or self-righteousness. That negative approach never works. Instead, we should say, "I love you. You're my friend. This is hurting you. Let me help." I have had friends do this for me in the past and it is the main reason I changed my behavior. They basically told me why I was wrong and how they would help me be better. And, I hated it at first. Then, it made me want to be better – for myself <u>and</u> for my friends. Today, I treasure the friends who love me enough to call out my vices and encourage my virtues.

So, in the end, I have a relatively simple set of criteria I look for in an authentic friend. This includes my family – they need to pass the test too.

1. They must like me;
2. I must like them;
3. They must actively strive to be a good (but not a perfect) person; and
4. They must hold me accountable with love and compassion and allow me to do the same for them.

There are plenty of awesome people out there who just don't like me enough to be friends. Perhaps I am not fun enough or perhaps we have dissimilar interests. I would like to be their friend, but it is not meant to be. They like other people better. That stings a little, but it's okay. I only need a handful, remember? Then, there are plenty of people who would like to be my friend, but I remain hesitant. That's okay too. We live in a world of over seven billion people. There are enough potential friends to go around. The third criteria, however, is the most important. This separates the wheat from the chaff for me. The people that I want to be friends with actively strive to improve their character. They are not perfect, and will never be perfect, but they consistently seek to be good. More on this when we get to Takeaway #5.

<u>Takeaway #4</u>: Our Implied Social Contract

Contracts are meant to control an uncertain future. People create contracts so they can rely on something happening at a certain time or over a period of time. Think about signing an apartment lease. You know that you will have a roof over your head for a year and the landlord knows that a specific rent will be paid. You are both better off because of the deal. The essence of a contract is that parties are bound by its terms. You either do what you promised or you are in breach. When you breach a contract, the other party has the right to get out – and generally they should. So, if you fail to pay rent for a few months, your landlord would be well served to ask you to leave.

Friendships are contracts too – just not the way we commonly think about them. There is no written document that comes with a friendship (hopefully). We don't sit down with our friends and list out the terms of our arrangement. Can you imagine if a new friend sat you down and said, "Okay, now that we're friends, we promise to hang out every Thursday through Saturday night. You are going to let me borrow your car and I will introduce you to my other friends. We promise to avoid lying to each other and gossiping about each other. Deal? Let's shake on it." That would be awkward.

Instead, authentic friendships operate under an implied social contract. This means that it's never written down or talked about. The friends just implicitly know and should abide by the terms. Under such a contract, friends promise to:

- Be honest, kind, and genuine
- Spend quality time (uninterrupted all the time by social media, etc.)
- Listen to each other's problems equally and have each other's back
- Go on adventures
- Honor trust and openly communicate
- Hold each other accountable with love and compassion
- Forgive
- Help improve each other's character and seek to be an ethical person
- Rush in during times of crisis
- Etc. ...

You can see that these promises are demanding. This is why you only need a handful of authentic friends. When people enter these contracts with dozens of others then promises are bound to be broken. But, if you start to build a few authentic friendships around these terms, they are very likely to last a lifetime.

What happens, though, when a friend starts breaking these promises? This happens all the time when two people interact closely and spend a ton of time together. It's human nature. What's hard is knowing when to leave the friendship. Let's just state it plainly – broken promises mean that your friend is in breach of the contract. Like any contract, you now have choices. You can stay in the relationship, address the issue, and try and work things out. Or, you can leave. But when should you leave? That is the topic of our final takeaway.

TAKEAWAY #5: DEMAND THAT YOUR FRIENDS BE GOOD, NOT PERFECT

This last takeaway evaluates expectations for our relationships. In other words, we need to assess the level of "amazing" we expect from these people. Oftentimes we set these expectations too high – especially for our kids, parents, spouses, boyfriends, girlfriends, and on down the line. Then, we are disappointed when these people fail to meet them. We put them on a pedestal on which they simply do not belong. I have seen many relationships disintegrate because one party demanded that someone else basically be perfect.

There is a certain irony here … none of us are perfect. How do I know? Well, it turns out that the average person farts many times each day. That's right, I said fart. In the constant quest to further knowledge, someone conducted a Fart Study. I would hate to be the graduate student who tabulated that data. Nonetheless, it happened. The study made clear that, on average, a person farts fourteen times a day.[109] That is nearly one fart for every waking hour of each day. Some farts move as quickly as ten feet per second.[110] And it turns out that men and women fart equally.[111] I am not sure how to say this politely, but this applies to you too! Some of you are proud right now and others embarrassed. All I know

---

109 *The Fart Facts,* http://zomoetdat.nl/thefartfacts.com/index.html (last visited September 7, 2016). The website is translated into four different languages. That speaks to the interest in the topic.
110 Ibid.
111 Ibid.

is that a perfect person would not fart. Right? Farts are socially unacceptable for many perfectly appropriate reasons.

So, every time you pass gas, you act imperfectly. That should be reason enough to give our friends and family a break. They fart too. They will mess up sometimes and break their promises other times. Please give them some rope as you would hope they would do the same for you when you mess up and break promises. No one is perfect.

The better approach is to demand that the people you let into your life earn their spot. They do this by actively trying to be good. This means that they actively try to be more honest, compassionate, dependable, humble, patient, and courageous each day. You should do the same. They will not always hit this mark, of course, but neither will you. This is a tough line to draw – when am I demanding perfection as opposed to when am I demanding a person be good? Just look to whether the people in your life are practicing their virtues consistently. Over time, this will become more intuitive.

Finally, I promised to discuss when you should leave a disintegrating friendship. These are the hardest questions I get on the road and in class. I waited until the end of this chapter to discuss this topic for a good reason – I remain unsure. Walking away from any serious relationship is a tough call – one of the toughest we make. But we can reason our way to some guidelines.

First, you must decide how much slack to give a friend or a family member. How many violations of the social contract are acceptable? For people who have earned a place in your life over a long period, you might want to give them more rope. For newer friendships, maybe a bit less. This is not about keeping score; this is about keeping your circle of friends tight and surrounding yourself with the best people possible. Remember, you will act like your friends act. If your friends cheat, you will cheat. If your friends lie, you will lie. But, if your friends are honest and kind, you will be honest and kind. If you seek fulfilling friendships, then you must hang around people who honor the terms of the social contract.

Second, you must decide whether you can see this person make some positive changes. I have found that people do not change easily and certainly do not just start seeking to be a good person very suddenly. Why? Because it's easier to lie than tell the truth. It's easier to cheat than be faithful. It's easier to be a flake than it is to consistently be there for someone. Sometimes a major life event will shock a person into a different approach to life. But, barring that, change is hard. No one wants to just walk away at the first sign of hard times. Remember, a real friend rushes in. But there is a point where you become a doormat. You can operate with too much compassion and this is unhealthy. Keep asking yourself whether you are acting compassionately or more like a doormat when you make these tough decisions.

Third, if you choose to leave, you must handle the break-up with class. You should tell your friends that you are walking away and explain why. Tell them that they are breaking their implied promises. They may promise to change and then the ball is in your court again (see the second piece of advice directly above). Do you sense that they will abide by the friendship agreement now or do they just want you to stay? These conversations are tough but they represent the high character way to end a relationship.

Please note that this also applies to family. Everyone, I repeat … everyone, must earn a place in your life. And you must earn a place in theirs. If a member of your family is not actively seeking to be good and continues to breach other parts of the social contract, then you can and should walk away. You should not be tied to a chronically bad person just because they are related to you. But, I would give serious grace here because most people desperately want their relationships with their family to be strong.

Application: Me Too

I went through this "should I end the friendship" dilemma with one of my friends from high school. For years, we hung out, took the same classes, studied together, crashed my car, went on double dates, and played basketball nonstop. These were the good days. We went our separate ways after high school because we went to different universities. This was before cellphones, social media, and email. It was much harder to stay in touch. But we reconnected in our thirties and started doing all the same fun stuff again. It was like old times. But now, I made a living as an ethics professor with a far different outlook on life than I had as a kid. My friend bristled at my newfound morality. He was acting no differently than he did back then and wanted his old friend back. He told me stories of cheating on his girlfriend on work trips and picking fights. He hung around a crowd of which I wanted no part.

Infidelity is one of the few actions that is always morally wrong. Think about it, there are plenty of valid justifications for unethical behavior – injuring someone in self-defense, speeding to the hospital with a sick passenger, or bribing a toddler to brush her teeth. However, it's impossible to justify infidelity; unfaithfulness is always unethical. I mentioned this moral truth with the tone of a know-it-all and came off condescending. I was frustrated. He responded defensively with the time-tested statement, "Don't judge me!" He warned me that, if I kept it up, he would stop confiding in me. And that's exactly what began to happen. Friendships based on dishonesty and concealment are doomed and I knew I had to make a choice. The social contract was broken many times over. We failed to communicate with respect. We were not honest and genuine with each other. The support system slowly disintegrated. I watched my friend grow less and less interested in becoming a more ethical person.

It was time to move on. I fretted about the decision for months before ending the friendship. I kept rushing in, but it didn't make a difference. He was not about to change and was, in fact, frustrated about how much I had changed. Unfortunately, through his actions outside of the friendship, he had no longer earned a place in my life. I felt myself become a less moral person every time we hung out and I was conflicted internally. I would wake up unhappy because of how I acted with him the night before. By the way, I never said anything to his girlfriend about my friend's unfaithfulness. Should I have told her? Was it any of my business? What would you have done?

Moving on from that relationship was incredibly difficult. I miss my friend. However, I needed to remove the bad influence from my life. I wasn't asking him to be a perfect friend because I certainly did not reciprocate perfection. But, I did ask that he strive to be a good person. Although ending a friendship is always a very difficult decision, sometimes the right thing to do is walk away. Though painful, in retrospect, this clearly was one of those times.

You will recall that people are happiest with a very small group of authentic friends. That circle is too small for a bad egg. And, my friend's choices could have harmed my other relationships. I needed to do better. I encourage you to do better too – move on from the friends who cause you to struggle and find that small group of people who are consistently there for you in the tough times, who make you better, and who walk with you down the often-arduous path of life. It is true that a person does not need friends to exist, humans can do that all alone. But they certainly need authentic friends to truly live, to thrive. Or, as C.S. Lewis brilliantly opined, "Friendship is unnecessary, like philosophy, like art … it has no survival value; rather it is one of those things which give value to survival." Thus, friendship is one of the three real rabbits worth the pursuit.

CHAPTER 10:

CHARACTER

---

*"People of character do the right thing even if no one else does,
not because they think it will change the world
but because they refuse to be changed by the world."*
— Michael Josephson

*Good character is more to be praised than outstanding talent.
Most talents are to some extent a gift.
Good Character, by contrast, is not given to us.
We have to build it piece by piece by thought, choice, courage and
determination."*
— John Luther

Your character absolutely counts. The only way to be authentically happy is to be an ethical person. There is not much room for disagreement. No one believes that liars, cheaters, and gossips are happy deep down. The same applies to cowards, traitors, or the most arrogant among us. The desire to be a good person is a real rabbit, a prerequisite to being authentically happy. But there is an obvious problem when it comes to talking about this subject – most everyone thinks that they are a high character person. Again, I don't necessarily doubt you. I just need to be thorough.

This chapter will discuss what it means to be a person of high moral character. We will then delve into three ethical decision making frameworks you can use every day to make character-based decisions. Before we begin, here is my working hypothesis:

People of high moral character act virtuously in public and private. They seek the greatest amount of good for themselves and others. They do things the right way because that is their duty and not because they want people to think they are a good or honorable person. Their decisions are consistently based on ethical guidelines as opposed to gut feelings. In this way, they become moral decision makers and happier people.

Raise Your Hand If You're A Good Person

From the outset, it is important to develop a baseline of where people fall on the character spectrum. If everyone is a moral actor, this chapter is a waste of time. To get an idea, I used to ask my audiences a series of important questions. I stopped doing this, however, because I was so shocked by the results time after time. Picture a room of one thousand people. I would stand on stage at the beginning of my talk and say, "Okay, there are a lot of you in this room. I would like you to raise your hand if and only if you believe yourself to be a person of high moral character." How many hands do you think went up? If you guessed one thousand, you are correct. Everywhere and every time. Think about it, you don't want to be the one person who keeps a hand lowered when everyone else has a hand up, right? So, the result became predictable, but I had a sense people were fibbing.

I would then say, "Great. I have one thousand hands to pick from and a microphone. I am going to choose someone from this group to define for everyone what it means to be a person of high moral character. So, if you don't really know the answer or are too scared to voice your opinion, please put your hand down." How many hands went down do you think? If you guessed one thousand, then you are correct again. I was shocked the first time this occurred but then these results kept happening, venue after venue. So, I just stopped asking the question. My baseline had been established. There is no way that 100% of the people we meet have strong moral character – even if they think they do.

The glaring problem is that people tend to overestimate their morality. Our perception of our character is a bit inflated. Don't worry though, you aren't weird – this is just human nature. Please answer the following questions quick-reaction style and see for yourself. Just note the first word – yes or no – that pops into your mind:

- Are you honest?
- Are you compassionate?
- Are you courageous?
- Are you dependable?
- Are you envious?
- Are you greedy?
- Are you self-absorbed?

Most people who answer these questions quickly and honestly say, "Yes" to the first four and, "No" to the bottom three. That's because we tend to think we are good without really delving into the details. This chapter will help you make sure your answers are accurate.

HOW CAN I MAKE MORE ETHICAL DECISIONS?

There are plenty of reasons why people follow the rules. Some people obey to avoid prison. This is better than nothing, I guess. Society is better off when people don't hurt each other and act fairly. However, being good merely to comply with the law is a moral minimum and speaks little of a person's character. The motivations are all wrong. You are not able to tell whether such actors are authentically happy.

Other people are good because they want to appear good. They know they need a positive reputation to attract a date, a spouse, some friends, and even business relationships. Few people want to hang around unethical people and no one wants to do business with a slime ball. So, some people are forced to fake it. To me, this is just as bad as acting ethically to avoid arrest. The intention is still off the mark. Again, you would not be able to consistently tell whether such actors are authentically happy.

Finally, there are the people who are good because they believe in living a life of high moral character. These people act ethically for a just reason. For some people, their motivation comes from religion and, for others, from their conscience or moral philosophy. Some people are motivated by all three. Regardless of the source, these people's intentions are in the right place. The real rabbit of character requires you to be one of these good-for-the-right-reasons people.

So, how does one who desires to be in the "good person" group get there? To be blunt … it's hard. I tell my students that there is no answer key, no book where you just turn to page 575 and locate the solution to your specific ethical dilemma. This is frustrating to people. They want clarity. The closest we can get to clarity in the ethics field are philosophical frameworks upon which people can build their ethical decision making skills. So, though I cannot give you a specific answer, I can certain tell you how to get to an ethically appropriate answer. In the end, it is enlightening to employ prominent ethical frameworks to evaluate our character. Using philosophy in this way oozes sophistication and the concepts are within your reach.

The problem with using frameworks as a guide is that obtaining consensus on the morality of decisions is a difficult exercise.[112] Ethics is not like law where a judge has rules in place to hand down final, binding verdicts on legality. The

---

112 *See* Manuel Velasquez, Claire Andre, et al., *Ethical Relativism*, SANTA CLARA UNIVERSITY MARKKULA CENTER FOR APPLIED ETHICS, http://tinyurl.com/y8huztx (discussing cultural differences in moral practices).

parties may not like the outcome, but the rules are accepted and the judge's decision, for the most part, is final. In the philosophical realm, a plethora of very different frameworks exist to evaluate decision-making from an ethical lens and people disagree bitterly on which is most appropriate.[113] What I can say with confidence is that the most prominent ethical frameworks roughly fall into five broad categories:

- THE UTILITARIAN APPROACH – which revolves around the idea that a moral action is the one that produces the greatest good for the greatest number of people
- THE RIGHTS APPROACH – which revolves around the idea that human beings deserve dignity; therefore, respect for and protection of rights matter a great deal when evaluating potential decisions
- THE FAIRNESS / JUSTICE APPROACH – which revolves around the idea that ethical actions treat all human beings equally. If people are treated unequally (which is inevitable from time to time), then they must at least be treated fairly based on some defensible standard
- THE COMMON GOOD APPROACH – which revolves around the idea that interlocking societal relationships form the basis of ethical reasoning; this means that our happiness is directly linked to the happiness of our communities
- THE VIRTUE APPROACH – which revolves around the idea that "ethical actions ought to be consistent with certain ideal virtues that provide for the full development of our humanity. These virtues are dispositions

---

113 *See Poll: Would you consider yourself more of a Utilitarian or Deontologist?*, ESCAPIST MAGAZINE, June 1, 2013, http://tinyurl.com/n442x4r (showing that fifty-one percent of respondents considered themselves Utilitarians and nine percent Deontologists; fourteen percent disagreed with both frameworks and twenty-three percent admitted that they had no idea what these terms mean) and Charles T. Schmidt, Ethical Decision Making and Moral Behavior, UNIVERSITY OF RHODE ISLAND, http://tinyurl.com/l6mhthg (last visited June 5, 2013) ("It is very difficult to define ethical behavior. Many definitions exist, but most depend on using some standard of ethical behavior from which to judge the individual's behavior. Any standard used is subjective and cultural in nature and subject to intensive debate.").

and habits that enable us to act according to the highest potential of our character and on behalf of values like truth and beauty."[114]

From these five, we will evaluate three ethical approaches - Utilitarian, Rights and Virtue. These are the frameworks which I believe prove most helpful in analyzing ethical dilemmas arising in our daily lives.[115] This is a thinking-cap type of chapter. You may have to read these sections a few times to understand the nuances. Each time you do, however, you will glean something new and valuable. As we proceed, try not to let the awkward and intimidating philosophy jargon mess with your mind. Please find comfort in the fact that these terms are awkward and intimidating primarily so that philosophy types can appear smarter than the average person and keep their jobs. Lawyers use complicated words for similar reasons – why else would you pay us $500 an hour to defend you? I will interpret these concepts as simply as I can. The idea is for you to get smarter not to get a headache. So, grab your thinking cap and let's go.

UTILITARIANISM

"Lying does not come easily to me. But we all had to weigh in the balance the difference between lies and lives."

– Oliver North (testifying to Congress after the Iran Contra Scandal)

---

114 *See A Framework for Thinking Ethically,* SANTA CLARA UNIVERSITY MARKKULA CENTER FOR APPLIED ETHICS, http://tinyurl.com/foj7e (last visited May 30, 2013).

115 The three frameworks utilized in this chapter stem from three of these five approaches; Utilitarianism stems from the Utilitarian Approach, Deontology from the Rights Approach, and Virtue Ethics from the Virtue Approach. Since I am a lawyer, I must add that interesting legal publications delve into these ethical theories from time to time. See, for example, Sherman J. Clark, *Law as Communitarian Virtue Ethics,* 53 BUFFALO L. REV. 757, 757 (2005) ("The governance and regulation of a community can and should be thought about in ways akin to the ways in which virtue ethics looks at the governance and regulation of an individual life.").

The Utilitarian approach – or Utilitarianism – is the most well-known of the "teleological" ethical frameworks. The word teleological comes from the Greek world *telos* which means goal, end, or purpose. People in this camp believe that the moral correctness of an action is directly correlated to the good produced by its goal or purpose, its *telos*. So, these people spend a lot of time trying to predict the end results of an action to determine whether acting that way would be ethical. In other words, the ends matter more than the means.

Utilitarians are therefore called "consequentialists" because the consequences matter most when deciding. The means – potentially lies, blackmail, bribery, or manipulation – used to obtain the desired end are far less relevant (and perhaps irrelevant to some in this camp). What matters is that good things happen in the end. To a Utilitarian, it would not matter whether someone rescues a drowning person to save that person or to steal his wallet. A life was saved and that is what matters most.

What a Utilitarian looks for is the degree to which the consequences produce the greatest utility (meaning good or well-being) for the greatest number of people. A decision-maker must place everyone on an equal playing field when making these decisions. Acting out of self-interest is a major violation of the theory. This is much different from a related Consequentialist theory called Ethical Egoism where an actor may act morally by being selfish. The only consequences that matter to an egoist are his own.

The Utilitarian decision-making process is relatively straightforward but still requires deep thinking and a somewhat accurate analysis of an unpredictable future. It proceeds in three steps:

1. The decision maker (i.e., you) must identify the various courses of action that you could perform when faced with an ethical dilemma;
2. Then, you must consider all the foreseeable benefits and harms that would result from choosing each course identified in step one; and

3. Finally, you must choose the course of action that provides the greatest benefits to the greatest number of people after all the benefits and costs have been considered.[116]

It is important to note that the chances or odds that each benefit and cost will come to fruition must be part of the analysis. One can ponder many tremendous benefits and horrible costs that have very little chance of occurring. Unrealistic expectations and worries should be highly discounted in a Utilitarian analysis.

There are two primary lenses focusing this evaluation process: Act Utilitarianism and Rule Utilitarianism. Act Utilitarianism applies the greatest good for the greatest number analysis to every single act that a person (or company / entity / decision maker) takes. The ethical action in each case is the one that brings about the greatest utility to all in that particular situation. This can become a very tedious task considering the many acts people undertake each day. Rule Utilitarianism, on the other hand, looks whether a general rule will bring about the greatest good. Rules that bring about utility are moral and should be put into effect and followed. Congress and other legislative bodies tend to act as Rule Utilitarians as they ponder which rules will make their communities more prosperous.

The so-called Classical Utilitarians are Jeremy Bentham and John Stuart Mill. Bentham formulated the first "systemic account of Utilitarianism."[117] He believed that "two sovereign masters: pleasure and pain" ruled human beings.[118] Therefore, good actions are those that tend to promote physical pleasure and bad actions are those that tend to promote physical pain. To Bentham, physical pleasures and pains were deemed equal to mental pleasures and pains and could

---

116 *See Calculating Consequences*, Markkula Center for Applied Ethics, August 1, 2014, http://tinyurl.com/zcchydu (discussing the idea that people use this type of moral reasoning frequently and stating:

When asked to explain why we feel we have a moral duty to perform some action, we often point to the good that will come from the action or the harm it will prevent. Business analysts, legislators, and scientists weigh daily the resulting benefits and harms of policies when deciding, for example, whether to invest resources in a certain public project, whether to approve a new drug, or whether to ban a certain pesticide.).

117 Julia Driver, *The History of Utilitarianism*, STANFORD ENCYCLOPEDIA OF PHILOSOPHY, March 27, 2009, http://tinyurl.com/hxmxvu3.

118 Ibid.

be quantified to assess which actions were moral.[119] It was John Stuart Mill, however, whose later interpretation of Utilitarianism gained the most traction.[120] Mill believed that mental / intellectual pleasures are intrinsically better than hedonistic or purely physical pleasures. To Mill, good actions were those that produce the greatest mental pleasure (happiness or well-being) and bad actions are those that tend to produce mental pain (unhappiness). Mill also looked to the quality of the pleasure and pain instead of merely the quantity.

The business context provides an appropriate vehicle to analyze the nuances of Utilitarianism. In business, the greatest number of people involves many stakeholders – employees, customers, shareholders, the families of the groups just mentioned, community members living nearby corporate property, and potentially society at large. Because this theory does not allow businesses to think of their interests above the interests of their other stakeholders, a Utilitarian analysis of business decisions often becomes very interesting. There are instances when revenue seeking will be unethical because the profit-generating activity will harm more people than the extra revenue benefits. This may be the last thing that a corporate executive desires to hear, but Utilitarianism makes the point very clear. However, profit is surely part of the utility that a business decision should consider along with other important benefits such as morale, workplace and community safety, stimulation of learning and creativity, environmental sustainability, and employee health.

---

119 In conducting this analysis of physical pleasure and pain, Bentham looked to its intensity, duration, certainty, remoteness, fecundity (basically, will more of the same pain or pleasure follow the current pain or pleasure), purity (basically, will the pleasure be followed by pain or vice versa), and extent (basically, how many people will be affected).

120 *See* Charles D. Kay, *Notes on Utilitarianism*, WOFFORD UNIVERSITY: DEPARTMENT OF PHILOSOPHY, http://sites.wofford.edu/kaycd/utilitarianism/ (last visited December 29, 2016) ("Although forms of utilitarianism have been put forward and debated since ancient times, the modern theory is most often associated with the British philosopher John Stuart Mill . . . who developed the theory from a plain hedonistic version put forward by his mentor Jeremy Bentham.") and *Utilitarianism*, WIKIPEDIA, http://tinyurl.com/7mt8v5o (last visited June 1, 2013).

A few key objections to Utilitarianism exist:

OBJECTION #1: *the consequences of an action are not always clear and it is exceptionally difficult to understand how these uncertain consequences will help or harm other people. Do people really want to base decisions on outcomes they cannot fully control or accurately predict?*

OBJECTION #2: *seeking the greatest good for the greatest number of people often leaves out minority groups and violates individual rights. For example, the Bill of Rights to the United States Constitution exists primarily to protect minority interests because a national government must function primarily on a Utilitarian basis (the majority rules). However, there is no equivalent to the Bill of Rights supplementing minority groups under Utilitarianism. Tough luck if you find yourself outside of the will of the majority.*

OBJECTION #3: *Consequentialist frameworks like Utilitarianism ignore the means to an end as morally irrelevant but this cannot be true.*[121] *Means, especially when injurious to others or otherwise unethical, should matter in the decision-making process. A person should not be able to use people as a means to an end even if that leads to a beneficial outcome.*

OBJECTION #4: *evaluating the greatest good for the greatest number of people is a time-consuming process. Many moral decisions require a much faster answer and people will not take the time to implement the calculus.*

---

121 *See* IMMANUEL KANT, GROUNDWORK ON THE METAPHYSICS OF MORALS 24 (T.K. Abbott trans. Prometheus Books 1988.) ("An action done from duty derives its moral worth, *not from the purpose* which is to be attained by it, but from the maxim by which it is determined, and therefore does not depend upon the realization of the object of the action") (emphasis added).

DEONTOLOGY

"Happiness and moral duty are inseparably connected."
– George Washington

"Do your duty in all things. You cannot do more, you should never wish to do less."
– Robert E. Lee

Deontology judges the morality of an action based on the actor's adherence to duty. A duty is a moral obligation that applies anytime and everywhere. Therefore, if you have a duty to be honest then you must be honest every time you consider lying. Your obligation to tell the truth remains regardless of the circumstances (a white lie versus perjury) or projected outcomes (the truth could cause an injury or a lie could save a life). Deontology is the opposite of Consequentialism. Consequences are irrelevant to making duty-based decisions because the future is too difficult to predict and control.

The key here is to analyze the "why" of an action (the means) as opposed to results (the ends).[122] Acting out of a sense of duty is the right thing to do. The emphasis is on the "*right* thing to do" rather than the "*good* thing to do." To a Deontologist, even tremendous amounts of good produced as the result will never justify immoral means. Finally, Deontology places emphasis on a person's duty as opposed to a person's motive.[123] For example, a person who tells the truth

---

122 *See Notes on Deontology*, WOFFORD UNIVERSITY, http://tinyurl.com/3ae3gjt (last visited May 31, 2013). *See also Terms In and Types of Ethical Theory*, DREXEL UNIVERSITY, http://www.pages.drexel.edu/~cp28/ethterm.htm (last visited December 28, 2016) (making the point via the following example: it would not matter if a drunk driver made it home safely after a long night at the bar – "driving drunk was still wrong because the intention to drive drunk was wrong (or to drink alcohol when one knows one needs to drive)" was wrong.).

123 *See* IMMANUEL KANT, GROUNDWORK ON THE METAPHYSICS OF MORALS (H.J. Patton trans. Harper & Row 1964, at 65), NIGEL WARBURTON, A LITTLE HISTORY OF PHILOSOPHY 116 (2011) (stating that morality for Kant "wasn't just about *what* you do, but about *why* you do it.") and NORMAN E. BOWIE, KANTIAN ETHICS, ENCYCLOPEDIA OF BUSINESS ETHICS AND SOCIETY 1499-1500

acts morally if and only if the truth is told because it is the right thing to do. Telling the truth is unethical if done to seek approval from others, enhance a reputation, or obtain a desired outcome. These are improper motives.

Immanuel Kant remains the world's most famous Deontologist. Kant believed that the humanity (loosely, the dignity) we all possess makes it immoral to use someone else *merely* a means to an end.[124] Under this formulation, it would be ethical to use people's talents for your own ends in situations like buying groceries, getting gas, or obtaining an education. This is ethical because these service providers also receive something valuable from the transaction. Using people becomes unethical, however, in situations where people are used merely as a means to someone else's ends. At this point, their humanity is brushed off as irrelevant. A Utilitarian may not see it that way if more "good" is produced by using someone solely as a means to an end – think about the government torturing a terrorist suspected to have the code to disarm a bomb counting down in Times Square. A Deontologist would avoid torture even though thousands might die.

Kant argued that people have the capacity to act from duty because we can reason.[125] This focus on cool rationality over emotion seems fair because some people possess less emotion than others. Your emotional quotient should not make you a better ethical decision maker. Emotions can also be dangerous because of their ability to cloud judgment.

(Robert Kolb ed. 2008) ("Kant is looking toward reasons rather than motivation in the psychological sense. An action is right if it is performed for the right reason and the person of goodwill is the person whose actions are based on or are in conformity with good reasons.").

124 *See Notes on Deontology*, above in note 11 and Robert Johnson and Adam Cureton, *Kant's Moral Philosophy*, STANFORD ENCYCLOPEDIA OF PHILOSOPHY, http://tinyurl. com/dejz25 (last visited June 1, 2013) (explaining that Kant did not:

[R]ule out using people as means to our ends. Clearly this would be an absurd demand, since we do this all the time. Indeed, it is hard to imagine any life that is recognizably human without the use of others in pursuit of our goals. The food we eat, the clothes we wear, the chairs we sit on and the computers we type at are gotten only by way of talents and abilities that have been developed through the exercise of the wills of many people. What [Kant's idea] rules out is engaging in this pervasive use of Humanity in such a way that we treat it as a mere means to our ends.).

125 *See Kant's Moral Philosophy*, *above in note 13* (stating that Kant "argued that conformity to the [Categorical Imperative] . . . and hence to moral requirements themselves, can nevertheless be shown to be essential to rational agency.").

Kant articulated these principles through his major contribu
Deontology – the Categorical Imperative (CI). The CI determines whether a
person has a duty to act or refrain from acting. In other words, the formula
declares how people, acting rationally, should behave.[126] An *imperative* is
an unavoidable obligation or an order.[127] The fact that Kant's formulation is
categorical means that obligations deemed to be duties under his rubric must be
performed by everyone, without exception, each time the obligation arises.[128]

Kant's CI declares: "Act only according to that maxim by which you can at
the same time will that it should become a universal law."[129] Kant's formulation of
a categorical imperative is a little clunky due to the philosophy-speak for which
he is infamous. But his theory is elegant when put into practice for most ethical
dilemmas. Translated to plain English, the CI contains three distinct steps:

1. **Define a maxim (a short, pithy statement or rule) that states your
   reasons for acting as you propose.** It is important to identify the action
   to be evaluated with some specificity, but it need not contain all the
   details. For example, "I may act dishonestly when lying would better
   suit my needs" is better than "I may be dishonest to the partners in a law
   firm about my expertise when lying will allow me to work on the most
   important case the firm has ever litigated." Less specific maxims will
   assist in universalizing the maxim – the work of step two.

2. **Can this decision be universalized?** If you can make an exception for
   yourself, you must be able to imagine a world where others always make
   the same exception for themselves. If this produces an irrational result
   (you cannot imagine such a world making any sense), you have what
   Kant called a perfect duty to avoid taking the exception. If you have

---

126 This is different from *hypothetical imperatives* which only require a person to act in certain
   circumstances. A good example of a hypothetical imperative would be, "If you want to
   avoid prison, don't steal." WARBURTON, *above in note 12*, at 118. Kant believed that
   "morality was a system of categorical imperatives" instead of hypothetical imperatives. Id.

127 *See Imperative Definition*, DICTIONARY.COM, http://tinyurl.com/me4gzwm (last visited
   May 30, 2013).

128 *See Categorical Definition*, DICTIONARY.COM, http://tinyurl.com/m4qj94c (last visited
   May 31, 2013).

129 IMMANUEL KANT, FOUNDATIONS OF THE METAPHYSICS OF MORALS 39
   (Lewis White Beck trans., Library of Liberal Arts 1959) (1785).

a perfect duty, you must act according to that obligation every time it arises. In the example above, step two entails asking whether the maxim of lying when it suits your needs can be universalized. If you are allowed to lie when it suits you needs, then you must be able to imagine a rationally functioning world where everyone acts dishonestly whenever lying suits their needs as well.

Such a world would not make any sense. People would continually be deceived; contracts and handshakes would have no meaning; and, eventually, people would stop believing each other. There is a strong chance that people would stop listening to each other's promises completely. It would not make sense to lie to others in such a world because it is irrational to lie to someone who is not listening and who wouldn't believe you anyway.

This new world would thwart your maxim of lying to suit your needs. It would never work. Additionally, by taking this exception for yourself, you treat people as mere means to your end and ignore the humanity of the people you deceive – an unethical action under Kant's Deontology. The answer to this second prong of Kant's CI proves that lying cannot be universalized and, therefore, people have a perfect duty to tell the truth even when lying would better suit their needs.

3. **Would you want to live in such a world?** This third step is only reached if you could imagine a world that still functions rationally when everyone is always able to take the exception you desire. Under these circumstances you must now ask whether you are willing to still take the exception for yourself and live in such a place. The lying example would not be analyzed under this third prong because the world would cease functioning rationally if people lied whenever being dishonest suited their needs. This was established under the second question.

However, there are other scenarios where a person would reach this third prong. Assume the maxim: "I need not give anything to charity when I am succeeding financially in life and others are suffering." After evaluating prong two, the decision-maker would conclude that the world would not cease to function rationally if no one ever gave anything to charity. Just because such a world can rationally exist, however, does not mean that it would be a hospitable place for a rational person to live. If a decision maker feels that such a world would be awful, then that person possesses an imperfect duty to give to charity. Imperfect duties like giving to charity generate praise when undertaken but fail to generate blame when avoided. This all leads to the conclusion that imperfect duties are those that a person cannot perform all the time (even the wealthiest person would run out of money eventually), but must be done some of the time and to a certain extent. The question is not whether a person should be charitable if financially capable, but rather, when that person must be charitable.

Do not forget that there is a final scenario that may arise under Kant's CI. There are situations where a rational person would have no qualms living in a world where the proposed maxim could be universalized. These cases provide neither a perfect nor an imperfect duty. In these circumstances, acting on the proposed maxim is morally acceptable.

There are a few key objections to Deontology as well:

OBJECTION #1: *the categorical imperative is just that - categorical - meaning that it "yields only absolutes."[130] A lie would always be wrong under this test even if were just a "polite lie" or a lie that saves someone's life.[131] This does not resemble the real world where the toughest ethical dilemmas involve grey areas.[132]*

130 *Notes on Deontology, above in note 11.*
131 Ibid. Imagine a scenario where your spouse spends hours getting dressed up for a night on the town. You do not like the ensemble. When asked, "How do I look?" you would be crazy to answer, "Terrible. I am not impressed." Is a lie here really unethical? Kant would say so because people have a categorical or perfect duty to always tell the truth in situations where it would be in their self-interest to lie.
132 *See* Larry Alexander and Michael Moore, *Deontological Ethics,* STANFORD ENCYCLOPEDIA OF PHILOSOPHY, November 21, 2007, https://plato.stanford.edu/entries/ethics-deontological/ ("There are situations - unfortunately not all of them thought experiments - where compliance with deontological norms will bring about disastrous consequences.").

OBJECTION #2: *Deontology has no clear answer on what to do when duties conflict. For example, what must a person to do when confronted with a duty to be honest and a duty to protect human life in a situation where a criminal asks if you have seen a potential victim run past. A person cannot choose the lesser of the two evils because that would be Utilitarian thinking about consequences.*

OBJECTION #3: *Do the duties that applied to generations past still bind actors in the twenty-first century? Values and thoughts about morality change drastically over time and Deontology struggles to keep pace.*

Despite these criticisms, as with Utilitarianism, many commentators apply Kant's Categorical Imperative to determine the morality of personal and professional decisions.[133]

VIRTUE ETHICS

"Excellence is an art won by training and habituation.
We do not act rightly because we have virtue or excellence,
but we rather have those because we have acted rightly.
We are what we repeatedly do.
Excellence, then, is not an act but a habit."

– Aristotle

---

133 *See generally* R. E. FREEMAN, STRATEGIC MANAGEMENT: A STAKEHOLDER APPROACH (1984) (discussing Kant's idea that people should not be treated as a means to an end in the context of business), Norman Bowie, *A Kantian Theory of Meaningful Work*, JOURNAL OF BUSINESS ETHICS, 17 (9/10), 1083–1092 (1988), Norman Bowie, BUSINESS ETHICS: A KANTIAN PERSPECTIVE (BLACKWELL PUBLISHERS 1999), Norman Bowie, *A Kantian Theory of Leadership*, LEADERSHIP AND ORGANIZATION DEVELOPMENT JOURNAL, 21 (4), 185–193 (2000) and A. Buchanan, *Perfecting Imperfect Duties: Collective Action to Create Moral Obligations*, BUSINESS ETHICS QUARTERLY, 6(1), 27–42 (1996).

Eudaimonia. This word roughly translates from Greek to mean human flourishing or success.[134] I like to think of it as overflowing happiness – the authentic kind that we seek on our journey through this book. Eudaimonia is not a temporary emotion. It is the lasting sense of well-being a person obtains from living a moral life. It is more than just physical or mental pleasure, which ebbs and flows. It is more than wealth, attractiveness, or popularity. We have seen that many people achieve these goals and yet fail to achieve authentic happiness. Virtue Ethics provides a framework meant to consistently generate this overflowing happiness.

Virtue Ethicists propose that achieving eudaimonia is the goal of every rational individual – whether or not the individual sees it that way.[135] People expend great energy – they exercise, invest, study, travel, work – all in order to achieve the Good Life. The problem to a Virtue Ethicist is that many people fail to equate the Good Life with the correct interpretation of eudemonia and, therefore, fail to flourish.

Unlike the teachings of Utilitarianism and Deontology, Virtue Ethics is not an action-guiding theory. Seeking the greatest good or determining duty is not the way for people to reach eudaimonia. The proper question is not, "What types of actions must I take to act ethically?" Under Virtue Ethics, a person must ask instead, "What type of life must I live to be a good person?" The idea is that someone seeking eudaimonia will have the disposition to make ethical decisions for the right reasons without the need for rules or action-guiding frameworks.

The key to Virtue Ethics is the development of this disposition – i.e., a good character. No one is born with a good character; you must work at it. The people you surround yourself with and your upbringing also play a big part. Once your character is developed, it must be exercised or it will fade. This is sort of like a well-chiseled physique fades in the absence of exercise. To develop

---

134 *See Eudaimonia Definition*, ENCYCLOPEDIA BRITANNICA, http://tinyurl.com/o2sg9d4 (last visited May 30, 2013) (defining the term as literally meaning "the state of having a good indwelling spirit, a good genius"). Another translation would be to possess a "good demon." *See Origin of Eudemonia*, MERRIAM-WEBSTER DICTIONARY, http://tinyurl.com/mup2hwx (last visited June 1, 2013).

135 There are very interesting works on Virtue Ethics; the most powerful are form the 1970s. *See generally* Philippa Foot, VIRTUES AND VICES AND OTHER ESSAYS IN MORAL PHILOSOPHY (1978), Peter T. Geach, THE VIRTUES (1977) and James D. Wallace, VIRTUES AND VICES (1978).

a good character, a person must habitually strive to acquire virtues and then act as a virtuous person would act in any given situation.

Virtues can be defined as:

1. Acquired character traits;
2. That make society better; and
3. Are universally admired and considered moral.[136]

To determine whether a trait is a virtue, I employ the *Ciocchetti Airport Test*.[137] Imagine you walk around any airport in the world and ask a random (hopefully rational) person whether it is good to be honest or compassionate. The answer will almost always come back, "Of course." The same thing would occur if you asked about benevolence, courage, and fairness. However, you are likely to receive many different answers if you ask random people at random airports if it is generally good to be wealthy or attractive. Some might answer yes and others no. A few might be unsure. This indicates that benevolence, compassion, courage, fairness, and honesty are virtues because everyone agrees that they make society better and are admirable and moral character traits. Wealth and attractiveness do not engender the same reaction. This response does not indicate that wealth and attractiveness are immoral. Rather, it merely indicates that these fakes rabbits are not virtues.

Virtue Ethics posits that virtues can be learned by practice and by associations. If you practice compassion, you will become more compassionate over time. If you are dishonest over time, you will become a liar. If you associate with people who lie, cheat, and steal, you will be more likely to lie, cheat, and steal over time. However, if you associate with people who are honest, kind, and compassionate, you are more likely to act that way. Habituating virtues over time will help develop a stable character and provide the best chance of attaining eudaimonia.

---

136 There are many similar definitions of the word virtue. See, e.g., ALASDAIR MACINTYRE, AFTER VIRTUE: A STUDY IN MORAL THEORY 190-91 (2d ed. 1984) (defining a virtue as "an acquired human quality the possession and exercise of which tends to enable us to achieve those goods which are internal to practices and the lack of which effectively prevents us from achieving any such goods.").

137 This is my creation so you will search in vain for the "Airport Test" of Virtue Ethics. But it works so let's go with it.

There are modern formulations of Virtue Ethics but none have gained the stature of the older, Aristotelian approach.[138] Aristotle, whose moral philosophy forms the foundation of all Virtue Ethics formulations, spent a great deal of time pondering and tweaking his ethical framework to determine what types of behavior would lead someone to achieve eudemonia, to live the Good Life.[139] To Aristotle, human beings have functions just as a knife has a function. A properly functioning, or good, knife is one that cuts well. A human being's function is to reason – this is what separates humans from other animals. Therefore, a properly functioning, or good, person can reason well. Aristotle believed that a person who reasons well will seek to live a character-filled life or the type of life that leads to eudaimonia. As with all formulations of Virtue Ethics, Aristotle's framework revolves around incorporating virtues into everyday actions.

This leads into Aristotle's concept of the Golden Mean[140] – the tool utilized to decide whether a person acts ethically. The Golden Mean is the middle ground between the excess and deficiency of any given virtue. The essence of every virtue lies at its mean. Take honesty, for example. A person who is consistently dishonest

---

138 The three most prominent today are the Eudaimonism, Agent-Based Virtue Ethics, and the Ethics of Care Approaches. Eudaimonism claims that there may be many paths to human flourishing but each requires a person to hone a good character to act morally. See generally G.E.M. Anscombe, Modern Moral Philosophy, in THE COLLECTED PHILOSOPHICAL PAPERS OF G.E.M. ANSCOMBE: ETHICS, RELIGION AND POLITICS (1981). Agent-Based Virtue Ethics holds that all that matters to determine whether a person acts ethically is that person's inner moral state at the time of the action; the state of affairs in the world surrounding that person (such as who may be hurt or which decision would produce the least harm) are not considered. See generally Michael Slote, Agent-Based Virtue Ethics, 20(1) MIDWEST STUDIES IN PHILOSOPHY 83-101 (Peter A. French et al. eds. 1996) and MICHAEL SLOTE, FROM MORALITY TO VIRTUE (2002). Finally, the Ethics of Care Approach stems from feminist philosophy and posits that morality must be understood in terms of relationships between people and can only be understood by people who care about the trials and travails of others. See generally CAROL GILLIGAN, IN A DIFFERENT VOICE: PSYCHOLOGICAL THEORY AND WOMEN'S DEVELOPMENT (1982) and NEL NODDINGS, CARING: A FEMININE APPROACH TO ETHICS AND MORAL EDUCATION (1984). There are also other, less popular, modern Virtue Ethics frameworks -- especially since the revival of this way of thinking in the twentieth century. See Nafsika Athanassoulis, Virtue Ethics: Internet Encyclopedia of Philosophy, http://www.iep.utm.edu/virtue/ (last visited December 28, 2016) (providing a good summary of modern Virtue Ethics theories).

139 *See generally* ARISTOTLE, NICOMACHEAN ETHICS (Robert C. Bartlett and Susan D. Collins trans. University of Chicago Press 2011) [hereinafter ARISTOTLE]. See also NIGEL WARBURTON, A LITTLE HISTORY OF PHILOSOPHY 9-14 (2011).

140 *See* ARISTOTLE, *above in note* 28, at 90-114.

is a liar whereas a person who is consistently too honest is blunt. True honesty lies at the mean of these extremes. A person whose character exhibits this deficiency or excess of honesty will struggle to find eudaimonia whereas a person habitually seeking the mean will become more honest over time. All virtues (including their deficiencies and excesses) can be plotted on the following spectrum:

FIGURE 1 – VIRTUE ETHICS SPECTRUM: HONESTY

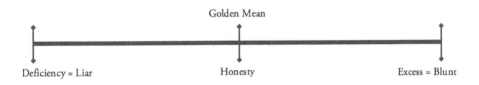

There are hundreds of virtues available for analysis under this framework.[141] You should pick a few and run them through the Golden Mean test in your life. Here are a few to start with: accountability, ambition, benevolence, confidence, courage, discernment, fairness, helpfulness, honesty, honor, integrity, loyalty, mercy, sincerity, respect, tact, and trust. The key takeaway from Virtue Ethics revolves around the idea that people who fail to act virtuously and habitually seek the Golden Mean will find themselves personally unfulfilled. They will also struggle to make ethical decisions at home and in the workplace.

There are a few key objections to Virtue Ethics:

OBJECTION #1: *the theory is not action guiding. Encouraging someone to act like a virtuous person is not as immediately helpful as telling someone to seek the greatest good or to run the decision through the Categorical Imperative to determine if a duty exists. This is too subjective and people may end up winging their decisions under Virtue Ethics under the assumption that they are acting ethically.*

---

141 *See List of Virtues*, VIRTUESCIENCE.COM, http://tinyurl.com/lpx6au4 (last visited May 30, 2013) (listing over one hundred virtues).

There is a response to this objection. Aristotle might argue that a virtuous disposition will lead you to moral choices just as often as following the Categorical Imperative (which also involves much uncertainty). Under the C.I. people must ponder whether they would want to live in a world where something does or does not happen. That assessment is subjective too. It is also very subjective to make a hypothetical analysis of the greatest good. How do you know for sure how people think of what's good in their minds? How do you know your decision will impact them in the way you envision? So, Virtue Ethics stands as good a chance as these action-guiding theories in leading you to a moral choice.

OBJECTION #2: *the theory does not tell people what to do when virtues conflict. What happens when someone desires to be an honest person as well as a loyal friend in a situation where a friend asks for unauthorized help on a test? Something must give, right? It appears that you can be either honest or loyal here but not both. Two virtues appear to be in conflict.*

There is a response to this objection as well. You might think about this scenario a bit differently. Upon first glance, this looks like a virtue conflict. But, after digging deeper, you might note that your friend is asking you to be excessively loyal here. That's outside of the Golden Mean. So, you can be honest and say no and, at the same time, not worry about being disloyal.

OBJECTION #3: *Virtue Ethics is subject to the criticism of Moral Luck. This is the idea that it is hard to hold someone morally accountable when the factors used to judge her actions are out of her control.*[142] *Virtue Ethics posits that habituating virtues depends somewhat on luck and being surrounded by virtuous people – especially throughout childhood. What about people who are surrounded by all the wrong influences (family, friends, and colleagues who do not act virtuously)? Does a person with such an upbringing even have the opportunity to become virtuous and, if not, is that equitable?*

As you may have guessed, there is a response to this objection as well. Perhaps Aristotle would argue that just because someone is subject to bad luck does not mean that they cannot act virtuously. They might have to try harder as this behavior will not come as naturally. But, all human beings have the capacity to live a virtuous life – even if it is more difficult to achieve.

Now you possess three guides to help you make ethical decisions. I am going to let you in on a little secret. There is nothing binding you to any particular framework. You can use all three interchangeably to help you. And, why wouldn't you? It would be blasphemy to take that approach if you were seeking your PhD in Philosophy. There, you pick one and seek to discredit the others. But, in the real world, I suggest evaluating all three and then deciding. Remember, we seek character here, not PhDs.

At the end of the day, remember how we think of people with high moral character. They act virtuously, whether or not someone is watching. They seek the greatest amount of good for the greatest number of people. And, they abide

---

142 *Moral Luck*, STANFORD ENCYCLOPEDIA OF PHILOSOPHY, April 10, 2013), http://tinyurl. com/3mecsah. The theory is relatively recent with the seminal articles on the topic written just over thirty years ago. *See generally* Bernard Williams, *Moral Luck*, in MORAL LUCK: PHILOSOPHICAL PAPERS 1973-1980, at 20, 20-39 (1981) and Thomas Nagel, *Moral Luck*, in MORTAL QUESTIONS 24, 24-38 (1979).

by a sense of duty. And, they do things the right way because that's their duty and not because they want people to think they are honest, courageous, and kind. They basically use these three frameworks to guide their moral decision making.

TAKE CARE OF YOUR COMPASS (CONSCIENCE)

I would like to end this chapter with a story that ties everything together. A few years ago, my wife and I took our three-year-old to Bermuda. Not the best idea as Bermuda sits in the Atlantic Ocean around 2,200 miles from our Denver home. But that happened. With little Sophie on board, there was not a ton we could do. It would be a waste of time to head to a nice restaurant or tour the historical sites. Those experiences go poorly with a toddler. You can go to the zoo anywhere so we decided to tour the Royal Navy Dockyard. This place stands out for many reasons. Built in the early 1800s, the British used this huge dockyard as a base after they were defeated in the Revolutionary War (or the American War of Independence as they call it in this British colony). Bermuda, it turns out, is strategically placed between Canada and the West Indies islands. British ships sailing to these places as well as to and from Europe would find safe harbor at the dockyard. There they could undergo maintenance and stock up on food, supplies, and weapons.

The guide told us about the captains of these ships in the 1600 and 1700s. These were highly skilled individuals who were responsible for many souls. The captain had to navigate the ship to shore or hundreds of hungry people would surely die. Once the shoreline disappeared, these captains were on their own. They had a map, the stars, and a compass. However, a map is only helpful if you know where you are. The stars work as a guide but only at night and in clear weather. That meant that the captain's compass was critical. A well-built compass is accurate all day long and regardless of the weather. It always points more or less to what sailors call the True North. These instruments were so accurate, even back then, that Christopher Columbus noted that the compass, "always seeks the truth."

Let's assume that you are selected as the captain of one of these seventeenth-century ships. You have three hundred souls on board and you are heading from Europe to North America. It is crucial that you hit Bermuda to restock and have your ship evaluated. You are issued a compass upon embarkation and head on your way. The shoreline disappears and now it is up to you. Let's say that a few days pass and you accidentally drop your compass to the ground. What would you do? I bet you would frantically pick it up, dust it off, say a little prayer, and go on with the journey. You would be more careful the next time, but the instrument would likely still work.

Let's assume now that you are a little clumsy. You keep dropping your compass. Now, it's fallen to the ground a dozen times. What would you do? Well, I bet you would frantically pick it up each time, dust it off, and say twelve little prayers. But now, you could not be so sure that your compass still worked. Its accuracy would be in question. Could it still find True North? You would be adrift with your fingers crossed hoping that it gets you close enough to hit Bermuda someday soon.

Let's assume now that you lost your compass one day. It fell to the ground, froze, got spit on, and was stepped all over. You notice it a month later and frantically pick it up. You dust it off and see that it's now cracked. You say a little prayer to no avail this time. Your compass is busted from all the neglect and in desperate need of repair. You still have a month at sea and you are now lost.

I tell this story and then ask people how they make moral decisions. Most tell me that their gut is their compass. They ask me if that is okay and my answer is … it depends on the condition of your gut. How have you treated it over the journey of your life? Does it work or is it worn down from neglect? Your compass is your gut, or better stated, your conscience. It starts out very accurate and then morphs based on the inputs you provide.

Remember how accurate your conscience was when you were six? When you lied at that age, it just felt wrong. When you sassed back at your parents or a teacher at that age, that behavior felt wrong. There aren't a lot of six year olds running around cheating in their elementary school classes. Why? Because their compass still points to its True North. Kids do not use ethical frameworks to make decisions. Instead, they always follow their gut and it generally leads them to a good place.

But have you noticed that, as we get older, our gut feelings become more suspicious. They are not as accurate because we realize that we can put our conscience on mute. In our teens, we start to justify our unethical behavior. We think things like, "I know I shouldn't lie, but I really want this person to like me." And then we hit mute. We go to school and think, "I know I shouldn't cheat on this test, but everyone else is getting ahead and I am less prepared." And we hit mute again. This constant muting of our conscience is why it is a lot easier for us to lie as we get older. It's a lot easier to gossip and be mean to people now. Many of us don't think twice about cheating in a classroom or on a person. Why? Our compass has been dropped again and again and it's started to lose its accuracy. When you see the big-time cheaters in life, whether it be in business, politics, or anywhere else, their consciences seemingly stopped working long ago. Their compasses are broken completely.

Due to this neglect, our conscience no longer speaks to us with the same strong voice. We have put it on mute a few times too many. It's a garbage in, garbage out system. Instead of hitting mute, we need to keep filling our conscience with good inputs. This is where the frameworks come in. Practice acting in this manner and your compass will become more and more accurate again.

Let me encourage you to work on your character. I promise to keep working on mine. Like contentment and relationships, this real rabbit is essential to your happiness. Once you have this down you can raise your hand in a room of one thousand people and confidently answer my question – what makes someone a person of high moral character. Start talking about the stuff we learned in this chapter and you will put on a show.

PART III:
Go

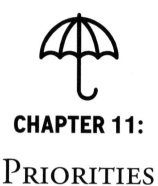

CHAPTER 11:

PRIORITIES

"Action expresses priorities."
– Mahatma Gandhi

*"In order to say yes to your priorities,
you have to be willing to say no to something else."*
– Stephen Covey

*"Decide what you want. Decide what you are willing to exchange
for it. Establish your priorities and get to work."*
– H.L. Hunt

Properly aligned priorities are essential to build an authentic life. People have nagged you about getting yours straight for years, right? Me too. It turns out that they were correct but likely for the wrong reasons. Older and supposedly wiser people would always tell me, "Corey, good things happen when you get your priorities straight." They would follow up with advice about finding a good job and working like a dog. "You'll have enough time for your friends and fun later."

All the while, I watched Hollywood glorify people who worked day and night. Hard workers must be doing something right to have their lives emulated in the movies. If I focused most of my time and attention on getting a good job and working hard, I thought, then my priorities would be straight. I would thrive. If you have read this far, you know how poorly that strategy worked out for me. Today, I take a much different, and much more beneficial, approach to my priorities and you should too. This chapter offers my roadmap.

Let's face it, priority conflicts are abundant and we allow them to linger. This means that people want to spend quality time with family, for example, but work too much. They want to exercise, but their time is gobbled up by a plethora of less-important tasks such as after-work meetings and social obligations. These conflicts lingered in my life as well. I desperately wanted to spend time with my family, but had an ever-present job. I was tethered to my phone and email. I wanted to learn Italian, but had to use my free time to catch up on sleep. I saw other people engaged in the same situation, struggling to escape.

My newfound real rabbits approach to life raised an immediate red flag – I needed to address my priorities. So, I dedicated time to answering some key questions. How can I better balance all my competing interests? Should I even try? Was one priority that much more important than any other? My heart seems to want them all, but I only have so much time in each day. So what needs to give? My efforts have been well worth the time. I discovered an approach to aligning priorities that maximizes happiness. This strategy works for everyone and involves no rocket science – just a pen, a piece of paper, and some courage.

The Most Important Advice You Read All Year

Pay close attention. This will be the most impactful advice you read all year! Trust me.

How can I be so bold?

My confidence comes not only from the drastic change in happiness I experienced in my life. It also stems from beta-testing this approach with many thousands of people over the past decade. The response has been overwhelmingly positive. I have huge boxes full of emails, letters, and cards thanking me for having the guts to talk about priorities in this way. These people tell me that aligning their priorities changed their life for the good.

My advice is powerful enough to have generated newspaper articles and stirred up significant controversy. Some love it and others hate it. It has earned me repeat speaking engagements at schools, corporations, and nonprofits. My approach to priorities has literally saved marriages and strengthened friendships (my intention) and has led to at least one divorce that I know of (not my intention; but, hopefully that couple is better off). It has led people to change majors and careers, quit jobs, or ask for a reduced work schedule. Some people bristle at this approach because it makes them very uncomfortable. So far, however, no one has told me that I'm wrong. Instead of challenging the approach, people either realize that my advice is accurate and continue to rationalize their choices or realize that my advice is accurate and make genuine changes.

I'll let you decide for yourself. Here is my controversial, happiness-maximizing approach to priorities:

You must align what you do in your daily life more closely with what your heart desires ... and do so as quickly as possible. Your heart should win because it knows better in this realm. Your heart is the most accurate guide to what you need to make you happy. This will take courage and will most certainly cost you something significant in return. But all the things worth having in life carry a significant cost. Trust me, the pleasure will greatly outweigh the pain in the long-run.

You might think that this sounds so simple, right? Just make the way you live your life line up with your heart's desires and do so right now. You would be mistaken. This advice is far easier to give than it is to take. Why? Because you might need to make big changes in your life like working less or at an altogether different organization. You might be forced to have tough conversations with your boss or put your phone and computer away when you get home and just be present with your family. You might have to mend some relationships with relatives and friends or spend more time volunteering instead of watching the football game. This advice might require you to exercise harder and eat healthier. None of this is particularly easy or on the path of least resistance. Now you can see why aligning your priorities takes courage.

The "Seasons of Your Life"

I am rarely surprised these days when I meet otherwise intelligent people who ignore their priorities. The required sacrifices are too difficult and cause too much brain damage. Instead, these people talk about "seasons of their lives." During these seasons, they ignore their heart and work very hard at an important goal – usually schooling or a career. They will do this "for a season" – until they graduate, get married, earn a promotion, make their first million, retire, etc. They argue that their priority mismatch will be short-lived. When the season is over, they promise to attack their priorities with a vengeance from further down the path to success. To them, this is just delayed gratification. They see this approach as honorable and deserving of respect. At present, however, they are mired in their goal-seeking and learn to ignore what their heart desires.

This is a dangerous approach. These so-called seasons tend to last much longer than anticipated and people do not just start caring about priorities out of the blue. There is no switch to flip upon graduation or upon earning a promotion where your family suddenly starts coming first. You cannot count on being able to turn off your bad habits so quickly and pick up better ones. You are much more likely to just continue down the same track you are on and find a different goal to chase for the next season of your life. It should come as no surprise that those with a priority mismatch are not all that happy. They will remain this way until their life gives their heart what it desires. Period.

Please keep in mind that, by moderating your season of life and seeking your heart's priorities, you likely will not be the best in your field or the richest person on the block. There is a cost to be sure. But, you will be happier and still be able to contribute greatly to a world that desperately needs your help.

One final point is worth mentioning. Research shows that you should also write these priorities down and engage some accountability partners. You are twenty-one percent more likely to achieve your priorities and goals if you write them down.[143] This written document (typed out or scribbled on a cocktail napkin – it doesn't matter) is akin to a roadmap that sharpens your priorities and focuses your mind. After that's done, you are thirty-three percent more likely to achieve your priorities if you share them and ask people to hold you accountable.[144] That all sounds reasonable. These studies were conducted under proper research standards by professionals with PhDs.

I decided to push the boundary and conduct my own informal study. I am not a PhD-trained researcher and I followed no professional research standards – shocking, I know. But, my results were just as telling. I found – just using a tiny bit of brainpower and some common sense – that you are zero percent likely to consistently align your priorities if you: (1) do not have any, or (2) just ignore your priorities for a "season." Any happiness will be fleeting as your heart loses again and again.

With all this in mind, this chapter seeks to convince you of the following five arguments:

1. Priorities matter greatly to your happiness … so discover yours by evaluating your heart's desires.
2. Priorities only bring happiness if your life aligns to your heart's desires.
3. You will find that people's priorities are very similar – most of our hearts want family near the top and work a bit lower on the list. We also want to spend time with friends and be / stay healthy.
4. There is no doubt that such a priority realignment will cost you as does everything worth having in life.

143 *See* Gail Matthews, *Goals Research Summary*, DOMINICAN UNIVERSITY WEBSITE, http://tinyurl.com/hfeyt8n (last visited September 3, 2016).

144 *See* Sarah Gardner, *Dominican Research Cited in Forbes Article*, DOMINICAN UNIVERSITY WEBSITE, http://tinyurl.com/hsfz58o (last visited September 3, 2016) and Gail Matthews, *Goals Research Summary*, DOMINICAN UNIVERSITY WEBSITE, http://tinyurl.com/hfeyt8n (last visited September 3, 2016).

5. Priorities are what you put first not necessarily where you spend the most time.

ARGUMENT #1: FOLLOW YOUR HEART ... TO AUTHENTIC HAPPINESS

Why do priorities matter so much to authentic happiness? The short answer is that properly-aligned priorities provide our hearts the real rabbits they desire unencumbered by the fake rabbits our minds tell us to chase. People are relatively simple creatures. We are driven by our hearts but ruled by our minds. Our hearts are emotional while our minds are rational. Our hearts can get us into trouble while our minds keep us safe.

Think about the potentially dead-end relationships we chase out of pure emotion. Our mind balances this infatuation; it urges us to be more logical and look for more suitable partners. Our mind moderates our heart and looks out for our safety and security. Life works well under this balance – except when it comes to priorities. For priorities, our heart is a far more accurate indicator of what we truly desire and where we should spend our time. Our minds fall prey more easily to the lies the world puts forth.

For example, the world tells us to chase wealth. Our hearts generally respond to this plea with a, "Whatever." Deep down, very few people care about being wealthy. Deep down, people just want to be happy. Our minds, on the other hand, think about all the things money can buy as well as the status and safety a lot of money provides. Our minds see other people chasing money and become increasingly competitive. Keeping up with the Joneses is a state of mind and not a desire of the heart. Our mind is tricked into thinking that money will bring happiness and so we work harder and harder for longer and longer hours. We are far better off following our heart here.

Again, the world tells us that looks matter. Our hearts often respond with, "beauty is skin deep." Our minds, on the other hand, are stimulated by the popularity and attention that comes with beauty. Our minds see other beautiful people and want to be more attractive. Our heart blows beauty off, but our minds chase. You get the picture.

Many may dismiss this as non-scientific, philosophical babble. And that may be true. The rest of this book is philosophical in nature, however, and still makes compelling and practical arguments. Not everything need be scientifically proven to be worthwhile. But, there is an emerging body of scientific knowledge that also backs up my theory. Scientists have found that our hearts are not just service organs pumping blood through our bodies. There are at least 40,000 sensory neurons that relay information from our hearts to our brains.[145] This has led "researchers to call the heart the 'little brain' and to coin the field as Neurocardiology."[146] Scientists have found that the heart affects our "mental clarity, creativity, emotional balance and personal effectiveness."[147] So, it seems as if our hearts may indeed have something to say about how to prioritize our lives.

Ponder your life for a moment. Isn't it true that you are happiest when you follow your heart over your mind, when you take a chance on a hobby, an adventure, or a job outside of your brain's comfort zone? Not unabated or blindly mind you; our hearts often run full speed ahead when it comes to emotion and we must exercise some discretion. We must be able to distinguish our actual desires from our emotional pleas. But, we are happiest when we let our hearts wander a bit and direct our paths towards our actual desires.

Try as you might, your mind does not control your happiness when it comes to priorities. Your heart does and, therefore, your heart dictates whether you are happy. Despite the truths contained here, many people continue to ignore their hearts and follow their minds regardless of the negative consequences. The path to authentic happiness takes a different track.

145   Dr. Joel Kahn, *7 Scientific Reasons You Should Listen to Your Heart (Not Your Brain)*, MIND BODY GREEN BLOG, December 16, 2013, http://tinyurl.com/oq27obc. (stating that Dr. Kahn has studied people's hearts for 30 years and "is the founder of the Kahn Center for Cardiac Longevity. He is a graduate Summa Cum Laude of the University of Michigan School of Medicine and is a Professor of Medicine.").
146   Ibid.
147   *Science of the Heart: Exploring the Role of the Heart in Human Performance: An Overview of Research*, THE HEARTMATH INSTITUTE, Vol 1 (1993-2001), http://tinyurl.com/jcvd8db (last visited September 4, 2016).

ARGUMENT #2: ALIGN YOUR PRIORITIES, CHANGE YOUR LIFE

Argument #1 made clear that our heart signals our priorities and our happiness depends on overcoming the resistance of our mind. Therefore, we must search and follow our heart to find out what it wants and then let that dictate how we prioritize our lives. This is the textbook definition of our authentic self. We then need to honor these priorities with our time, energy, and attention. But this transition is where most people fail. The get scared and fall back to following their mind's priorities. So, I will share with you what I tell my students when they need to grasp important information – time for some homework.

I made it all the way to CHAPTER 11 without assigning homework. Not bad for a college professor. But now you are bit more enlightened. Now you understand the type of foundation you must develop to be authentically happy. You know which rabbits to chase in life and which to avoid. You are beginning to understand the importance of priorities as the linchpin to happiness. So now, it is time to apply this knowledge to your life.

This is the ideal type of homework assignment; the kind that doesn't take too long to complete and has the potential to make a huge impact in your life. No one will collect it. There is no grade. Only you will see your answers. My advice, however, is to hang this on your refrigerator when you finish. That is where all the important things in our lives go and this assignment is critically important. I also believe that, when it's completed, you will share your results widely. My hope is that you encourage the people you love to do the same homework.

YOUR HOMEWORK: PART 1 | GET AN ACCURATE REPRESENTATION OF YOUR HEART

Take a piece of paper and draw a vertical line down the middle. On the top left side draw a heart. Then number the ten lines underneath your heart (see the table below). On each of these lines, list your priorities, in order, one by one as your heart desires them. In other words, in a perfect world, what would you do first? What would you do third, fifth, eighth, etc.?

Here are the most common priorities people list on this side – family, friends, religion, work, school, and health. I bet that similar terms came to mind for you. How do I know? As I have said, we are all beautifully, equally human when it comes to what we seek in life. We all want contentment, relationships, and character. And, it turns out, that we all want similar things on the top of our priorities list. Where we differ in our lists is on the margins. Some of us will put rock climbing on the list, others opera. That is fine; this is your list and it should reflect your personality.

PRIORITIES IN YOUR HEART

	My Heart
1.	Immediate Family
2.	Religion
3.	Extended Family
4.	Friends
5.	Work
6.	Health
7.	Service
8.	Travel (for fun)
9.	Reading
10.	Woodworking (or any other cool hobby)

Notice that I only allow you ten lines. This is intentional and may not seem like very many priorities. However, ten priorities are more than enough to make a person happy. The adding on of priority after priority explains why our paintings give us headaches (see CHAPTER 8). Remember the barrenness of an overly busy life? We just do not have time to prioritize more than ten things. This is especially true as we mature and our tasks increase in difficulty and importance (think jobs, kids, marriages, friends, community service). This stuff matters a great deal and so some other, less important, stuff has got to go! If you cannot figure out what to delete, then list all thirty or so things that matter to you right now and begin to pare them down to ten.

The only strategy I disallow is combinations. You cheat if you combine family with friends to obtain one more spot on the list. Same with combining your job with a hobby or your job with travel to obtain one more spot. When you combine priorities, both tend to get short-changed and you prioritize neither. Other than that, this list is yours to craft. This is the fun part; take your time and concentrate. Your homework is about to get a lot harder.

YOUR HOMEWORK: PART 2 | GET AN ACCURATE REPRESENTATION OF YOUR LIFE

On the top right side of the same piece of paper, paste an actual picture of yourself (or draw a stick figure if you're lazy). I want this figure to look like you. That way it will be harder to ignore your priorities as you look back at yourself from the fridge. Now, number the ten lines beneath your picture. This side of the chart is reserved for your priorities as you currently live your life. This is where you must be honest. This is where the rubber meets the road. Look back six months or so and list what generally came first through tenth in your life. So, for example, if you consistently choose to miss dinner with your family to work, then place work higher than family. If you consistently prioritize work above your health, then place work higher. If you sleep fitfully or for less than seven hours a night, put health lower. You get the drift.

PRIORITIES AS YOU <u>CURRENTLY</u> LIVE YOUR LIFE

My Life | [insert your selfie here]	
1.	Work
2.	Immediate Family
3.	Health
4.	Extended Family
5.	Religion
6.	Friends
7.	Reading
8.	Travel (for fun)
9.	Service
10.	Woodworking (or any other cool hobby)

Note: You will be tempted to cheat here. No one wants to admit that their priorities are all screwed up. You don't have to be a genius to see the path I am leading you down to complete this assignment. So, as you finish your right side, here is a simple rule to contemplate: If you cheat on a homework assignment given to you by an ethics professor, in a book all about ethics meant to make you a better, happier person … you go straight to hell. I'm kidding, I think. Who knows really. All joking aside, after this step you will end up with ten priorities beneath your picture. What you will see is that most of the words from the left side of your list reappear on the right side – just in different order. We have established that life is not good when you heart wants something that your life doesn't provide, so . . .

YOUR HOMEWORK: PART 3 | CONNECT YOUR LINES & DISCOVER HOW MUCH WORK YOU MUST DO

Time for the results. You need to connect similar priorities with a line across your chart. So, connect family to family and work to work. Draw lines between health and hobbies on both sides. If something makes one side of the list but not the other, then draw a line that runs off the page.

Afterwards, you need to step back and carefully evaluate your lines. If you have a lot of horizontally parallel lines, then good work! Even if I don't know you that well, I would place a bet that you are an authentically happy person with those results. However, if your lines are diagonal – either diagonally crossing or diagonally parallel – then, "Houston … we have a problem." If these diagonal lines are all I saw and I didn't know anything else about you, I could surmise very accurately that you aren't all that happy. And how could you be? Your life is not providing the things your heart desires. It's as if the following dialogue occurs in your subconscious:

YOUR HEART: "I desperately want family to come first."

YOUR LIFE: "Too bad. You get work."

YOUR HEART: "But, I don't want so much work. In fact, I want to travel more with my family."

YOUR LIFE: "Too bad. You get work. That's the way it must be because [insert some fake rabbit chasing reason here like money, pride, renown, or season of my life]."

And we wonder why sixty-seven percent of Americans don't wake up happy. It's not just you. This next chart represents how my chart looked the day I heard John Bogle speak on real rabbits. I was a mess. Look at all the diagonal lines. My heart and my life were at an almost total disconnect. Something had to change.

MY PRE-REAL RABBITS, PRIORITIES HOMEWORK ... NOT GOOD

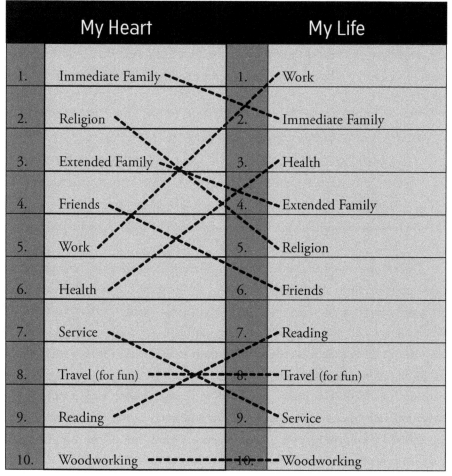

My Heart		My Life
1.	Immediate Family	1.	Work
2.	Religion	2.	Immediate Family
3.	Extended Family	3.	Health
4.	Friends	4.	Extended Family
5.	Work	5.	Religion
6.	Health	6.	Friends
7.	Service	7.	Reading
8.	Travel (for fun)	8.	Travel (for fun)
9.	Reading	9.	Service
10.	Woodworking	10.	Woodworking

As the first part of this book demonstrates, I was at a crossroads. My heart was getting nothing it wanted. My heart asked for family and I gave it work. My heart wanted to go to church and I gave it more work. The only reason health was so high on my chart was because I needed to work out to decompresses from my hours and hours at work. You can clearly see what dominated my priorities and therefore my time. This was not what my heart wanted and I had to quit my job. I was on the verge of a breakdown.

ARGUMENT #3: PUT FAMILY FIRST

So, what does a heart desire? Welcome to yet another controversial part of the book. I get in trouble for making the point I am about to make. It is certainly not something you expect to hear from a business professor. But, I say it anyway because I know it to be true and I have tenure so it is tough for them to fire me. Here we go:

Your career, education, or professional accomplishments should not make your top three priorities. Those spots are reserved for human beings (this applies to everyone) or religion (this applies to many) and not work or school — which should come fourth.

That's right, I said it. And I mean it. The top three spots in your priorities chart are reserved for the most meaningful things in life. This means that your work and education should come fourth. Notice that I said fourth and not lower. We live in a world that desperately needs your help. We need you to plug in and most people do this via their education and career. There are very few jobs in this world that allow you to prioritize them tenth on a list of ten. That is not what I ask. In fact, I would not have a platform to write this book were it not for my education and experience and all the hours and hours of my time all that took. Professional accomplishments make the world better; but, these things should never be prioritized ahead of the people you love and / or your faith.

This is just the plain, good old-fashioned truth. How can I be so sure? I have spoken to well over 500,000 people over nearly a decade. Yet, I have never run into one person who puts his or her job first who is truly content and happy. Have you? The same goes for education. Now, don't get me wrong, I have met a ton of people who prioritize work and are rich. I have met plenty who have their own yachts, planes, and helicopters. In America, you can put work first and find worldly success. That's the beauty of this country. The problem is no one ever tells you to stop or that your chase cannot make you authentically happy.

No one ever comes up to me and says, "You know what? You're wrong about all this priority stuff. I work 80 hours a week and I am so happy. My kids don't really know me, but I really enjoy my life as is." That conversation just does not happen - zero times in half a million opportunities. What does happen, however, is more concerning. Successful professionals approach me after my speech – usually it's one of the bosses. They don't want to say anything in front of their subordinates, so they ask to speak with me off to the side (kind of like the popular kids after I speak at a high school).

They say something to the effect of: "You know, you're right. I work 80 hours a week and I'm miserable. My kids don't run up and hug me when I get home or they are asleep by then. I am blowing up my marriage and I am close to becoming a full-blown alcoholic. To make matters worse I find myself depressed, sometimes enraged, and I sleep terribly. Can you help me?"

I respond with something to the effect of: "I understand and am so sorry to hear that. I must say that I hear this all the time from successful people like yourself. Let me just be blunt and say that the way to fix all this is to go home and fix your lines."

Their responses veer off a bit depending upon who I am talking to:

EXECUTIVE #1: "I know you're right, Corey. But, if I do what you say my stock options won't vest."

This is the money is hard to come by counter-argument.

EXECUTIVE #2: "I know you're right, Corey. But, I am one of the few women at this level in this company. I am good at this job and getting promoted fast. But, if I do what you say I will not advance quickly, if at all. This is a chance for a woman to make news here."

This is the taking one for the team counter-argument.

What these people are basically saying to me is, "I know you're right about my priorities. But, if I do what you say, it will cost me." And that's true. But it is well past time for the cost to come out of our careers instead of our marriages, families, and other important relationships. After all, that is what our hearts always prefer.

BEYOND A REASONABLE DOUBT

Let me see if I can prove to you that priorities matter greatly to your happiness in a different way and like a good lawyer – beyond a reasonable doubt. My wife is a trauma surgeon. She sees people in the process of dying, whether it be a motorcycle crash, a car crash, or a bad fall. She is a compassionate soul and talks to her patients at their bedsides. These people open up and confide in her. In all this time – over a decade – not one person has ever said to my wife, "Well doc, I'm dying. I just wish I would have worked a little harder. It's my one regret." They never wish for more money, or that they were better looking, or that they had nicer stuff. They do not lament the fact that they did not party more, travel more, or smoke more pot (sorry students).

They basically say, "Doc, I'm dying and I wish I would have been a better person – a better mom or dad, a better son or daughter, a better friend." The only time work comes up is when they say they wish they would have been a better colleague.

These responses got me thinking about law. In the law, there is a concept called hearsay. You've likely heard of this (or seen it on *Law and Order*). Hearsay is when I go into court and testify about something that someone else said. This is rarely allowed because such testimony is not very reliable. Remember the game of *Telephone*? One person whispers a few sentences to the next person in the circle. This person is supposed to then memorize what was said and repeat it to the next person line. And on and on it goes, all the way around. Typically, by the time it reaches the third person or so, the content is far from what was originally whispered. By the end it's completely different. The legal community has found that a better approach to garnering accurate testimony is to find the speaker, put her under oath and let her tell the court what she said. Her own testimony under oath is far more reliable because she is legally bound to tell the truth and must face the crucible of the other side's attorneys.

But, sometimes it is difficult to locate the speaker and compel her to testify. Witnesses disappear and, from time to time, they die. These deaths are nothing sinister (we hope) but witnesses are often unavailable. The show, however, must go on – justice must be served. So, judges and lawyers long ago crafted a few exceptions to the hearsay rule. One is called a Dying Declaration. If I hear you say something while you are in the process of dying, I can often testify about it under oath. I can repeat what you said in that situation. Why? Because what people say when they are dying tends to be true. People just don't lie in these situations. Some feel like they have nothing to lose when death is imminent. Others get religion in their dying moments and do not want their last act on Earth to be a lie. Whatever the reason, dying people consistently tell the truth. Therefore, the law allows me to testify about what I heard in these cases.

With all this in mind, let me be very clear. **Until people on their deathbeds start telling my wife that they wished they would have worked harder, had more money, been better looking, chased more fake rabbits … I'm right!!!** These are accurate statements said by people who are critically reflecting on a life that is about to end. They have nothing to lose by telling the truth. They wish they would have put people first and soon they won't have that chance.

Let's face it, you know that I'm right about this. So, I repeat to you what I tell major executives of huge companies when they ask how to be happier. Go home and fix your lines. Your happiness literally depends on it.

<u>ARGUMENT #4</u>: THE COST OF PRIORITIES

We have established that getting your priorities straight is crucial if you seek authentic happiness. But, the process is certainly not free – it will cost you. Some things just must give. As I mentioned earlier, each place on your list can only hold one priority. It is human nature to give up on goals that come at too great a cost. So, this is where I begin to lose people.

In an effort to keep you on board, let explain how my properly aligned priorities list has cost me. There is little chance that I will never teach at an Ivy League school. That career path is a professor's dream – to end a career teaching brilliant minds at schools of that caliber. The students would be smart, hard-working, and engaged in their studies. I would be surrounded by geniuses, have resources at my fingertips, and never worry about accreditation or enrollment numbers. My classes would be full. I would love to teach at an Ivy League school.

But these institutions are never going to hire someone who prioritizes his job fourth – especially someone who stands on stage and encourages others to do the same. My priority alignment has cost me a certain level of career advancement.

My priority alignment also continues to cost me at my current job. There is an award at my school called the *Award for Excellence*. It goes to the professor who is always there, burning the midnight oil. Winning this award requires you to team up with your colleagues, often after hours, and do something big that makes the College a better place. I would love to win that award. Who wouldn't want to make an academic environment better for the students? The problem is that I am rarely even nominated. Why? Because, relatively early each night, I head home to have dinner and hang out with my family. I leave while others work. Being home with my family is a higher priority for me and will likely cost me the joy of ever winning the *Excellence Award*. My choice comes at a professional cost.

But let me make a promise to you. Though I may never teach at Harvard or win major awards, I am the happiest married man at my place of employment! I am trying to be the best dad there too. My students think I am a great professor. I know that I am not as good as I could be if I prioritized my job first. That much is certain. I would have three times as many articles published. I could travel to speak more. But, I am still very good at my job and I get to work at a wonderful institution. Prioritizing family first doesn't mean I cannot put in the time it takes to excel at work. I can't tell you how many times I have put the girls to sleep and then worked until two in the morning. All of this is the high price I pay for my priorities being aligned. I encourage you to pay this price as often as possible, however, because the reward is a happier life.

ARGUMENT #5: PRIORITIES ARE WHAT COMES FIRST

Here is my final argument on this important topic. This one will soften the blow a bit. **Priorities are not time spent, they are what come first.** In other words, the time you spend on any given task does not necessarily determine its ultimate rank on your list. Instead, your top priorities are what you do **first**. They are the things that should always get done regardless of how busy you are.

For example, my students lament that they do not have time to prioritize their families. College is just too time-consuming and it is hard to engage in family traditions, go home from time to time, or even call their parents regularly. They experience too many new forces pulling them in different directions. College is more demanding in this way than high school. They have also over-committed to many different student groups. They feel like missing a weekend of going out to go home will come back to haunt them academically and socially. All this over-programming tips their priorities chart off balance. But, there is an easy solution to this problem if they truly understand how priorities are supposed to work. Here is what I tell them.

You can still socialize, study, and volunteer while also prioritizing your family. When you wake up, call your dad. Tell him that you love him and talk about what you are studying this week. Ask him how he is doing and plan a time to connect in person. This doesn't have to be an hour-long conversation, but it should be meaningful because that's what your heart desires. Then say goodbye and hang up. Okay, that's done. Now that your dad has been prioritized, call your mom. Tell her about the schedule of classes you might enroll in next term and about the people you are meeting. Ask her how she is doing and plan to connect in person soon. This doesn't have to be an hour-long conversation either but, again, it should be meaningful. Then say goodbye and hang up. Okay, that's done. Now that your parents have been prioritized as your heart desires … go to the library and study all morning if you must.

You can safely study for hours more than these phone calls take because that's not the point. The idea is that the phone calls happen first. Students should never get so wrapped up in school (which they tell me is a lower priority) that they neglect their top priorities. Then, I tell my students that phone calls are a good start but they aren't enough and they should go home and skip some parties from time to time. The same silly things will happen at parties the next weekend. It is important to miss some of this and reconnect with family if that's what your heart desires. So, as you can see, priorities are about what comes first and not necessarily time spent.

The professional world is much the same. Any job worth having requires a ton of time and attention. It is key to remember that you can work long hours, just not at the expense of your family and other priorities. Your employer is not your master and, per the Thirteenth Amendment of the U.S. Constitution which bans involuntary servitude, they cannot make you stay. You might need to push back some and tell your employer you promise to get the rest of your work done later or from home.

So ... Must I Quit My Job?

This leads me to the end of the chapter and one of the toughest questions I am asked on the road. It involves work as a priority and goes something like this:

So, I work a ton and don't spend as much time with my family and friends as my heart desires. Are you telling me I need to quit my job?

My answer is always the same ... it depends. The bottom line is that you need to work in an environment where employees have the freedom and bandwidth to get and keep their priorities straight. You need a job where your heart can get what it desires. So, this might involve you changing jobs.

At my law firm, it was put work first or get fired. There was no real freedom to re-prioritize. If I told them that I wanted to be home for dinner with my family every night, they would have laughed in my face. Not even the most senior people did that. And, even when I got home, my job took so much from me during the day that I lacked the energy to spend time on my other priorities. I was exhausted.

Let me tell you a story from my lawyering days to put all this in context. We were in the middle of a big transaction like we always were. A senior associate asked a partner if he could leave and come back later that evening. His son was having a birthday party. I will narrate the ensuing, very disturbing, conversation:

ASSOCIATE: "Is it okay if I go home for a few hours to spend some time with my son on his birthday? My wife has planned a little party. I'll just go for a few hours and speed back. I'll stay later all week to make up for it."

PARTNER: "I just cannot afford for you to go. There is a lot of work to do and it's getting late. The client expects another memo from us in the morning."

ASSOCIATE: "Please. It's just a few hours. It would mean a lot to me, my wife, and my kid."

PARTNER: "How old is your kid anyway?"

ASSOCIATE: "He turned three today."

PARTNER: "Well then what are you so worried about? He won't remember if you're not there anyway."

End of conversation. I remember doing a double take upon hearing the end of this dialogue. Did that just happen? Unsurprisingly, the associate stayed, prioritized work, and missed the party. He was prioritizing his chance to make partner in a few years at this prestigious law firm. You cannot make the partners mad too often and then be voted into the club. This is what the partner was making clear in that conversation – leave and your chances of getting promoted decrease. A three-year old's birthday party was not going to interfere with that goal.

For the next month or so, it was painful to work for this associate. He was moody and depressed. I've rarely seen someone look so down in the dumps. There was no cheering him up. You could see in his face the strain his misaligned priories placed on his marriage and relationship with his son. And seriously, even if the son never remembers that his dad missed his third birthday party, his dad always will! I cannot say that I would have made a different decision at that point in my career. You get locked in a trance. I felt like I was flying an X-Wing fighter jet away from the Death Star but they had me locked into their laser beam. It was tough to pull away. That associate needed to eject rather than get pulled further in. But he didn't have the courage, it's scary out there.

So, the answer to whether your misaligned priorities mean you should quit your job is sometimes, "Yes." You might have to change jobs or even careers if your current situation skews your priorities off balance consistently and you lack flexibility to give your heart what it wants. Something had to give in my life and I resolved to not let it be my family and health anymore. I had to quit my big-time legal career because putting that job fourth would have earned me a pink slip.

For the rest of you who don't have an all-consuming job, however, the answer is a bit different. Most times you can push back a bit with your boss. You can ask to take some work home to do after family time. You can come in a little earlier and you can always be more efficient. If these offers are continually rejected, then you might have to quit.

If you are the boss, try and make your firm a more family-friendly place. Why? Employees with misaligned priorities will be unhappy and less satisfied at work. They will carry their stress into the office. This type of stress is contagious and decreases productivity and morale office-wide. Find a way to accommodate your employees' priorities while making sure they hit their productivity goals. It's okay to allow their job to come fourth – that's still really high on the list.

CONCLUSION: OFFICER JEFF JUST LEFT

Let me sum up this chapter with a heart-warming story that places all five of my arguments for priority alignment in perspective. A few years ago, I was invited to speak to a large room of police officers in the Colorado mountains. It was a mandatory, week-long training retreat. There must have been five hundred uniformed officers in the room. These are always some of my best audiences. I preach to the choir with law enforcement. Afterwards, a line formed to talk with me and get an autographed book. Near the end of the line, a distraught looking officer approached. He waved off the book and seemed to have little interest in talking to me for long. I could tell he had something important to tell me. The conversation was intense and proceeded like this:

OFFICER: "I have something to tell you. I have a buddy named Jeff. He's on the auto theft investigation team with me. He was in room and listened to you talk about priorities and then decided to leave the conference. He went home."

ME: "Home?"

OFFICER: "Yes, home. We are supposed to be here all week. This is mandatory training. People are on edge because we've all been working overtime lately. There is a lot of gang activity surrounding auto theft. It's a dangerous job and we need this training to stay up to date and to bond as a team. Anyway, Jeff might get fired now because of you. No one just leaves until the Chief tells us to leave. This is the first day of the conference for crying out loud."

ME: "That does sound bad. Why would he leave because of me?"

OFFICER: "Jeff heard you speak and then went home to fix his marriage."

He walked away still agitated but I got goosebumps. This was my priority alignment theory at work in the real world. The chain of events was simple to deduce.

1. Officer Jeff was unhappy.
2. He realized that he had been working too hard and that his marriage was suffering. His heart wanted his marriage to come first but his demanding and dangerous job kept interfering.
3. I assigned him homework in my talk and he started to complete it in his head.
4. He filled out his chart, saw a bunch of diagonal lines, and decided to make a change … right away.
5. So, he left.

I assume that he was under no impression that leaving this required training was okay. He knew it would cost him – maybe even his job. But he left anyway. His marriage had to come first again in his life because that's what his heart was screaming. He could have put it off until the end of the week. But, he was trying to realign his priorities … right away. And when he came back to the training that week, I bet he was a better cop. A happier home life will always lead to a better and more productive work life. It's nearly impossible to leave the stress of a crumbling marriage at home. His leaving was a win-win for his family and the police force.

There is a huge caveat though. There is also a chance that Officer Jeff got fired for leaving without permission. I have no idea as I never had the chance to meet the man – he left without getting a book. It would be a terrible idea for the Chief to fire someone for leaving under these circumstances. However, not all the people that make hiring and firing decisions chase real rabbits. They might see work as the only acceptable top priority. Let's face it, losing a job is a risk that we all run when we let our heart dictate our priorities. It's not the way I would set things up if I were in charge, but it's the way the working world currently operates. Fired or not, I have a feeling that the courageous Officer Jeff will land on his feet … with a stronger marriage and a happier heart.

CONCLUSION:

SHINE

"Shine.
Make 'em wonder what you've got.
Make 'em wish that they were not.
On the outside looking bored.
Shine."
– Newsboys

"Drench yourself in words unspoken
Live your life with arms wide open
Today is where your book begins
The rest is still unwritten."
– Natasha Bedingfield

John Wayne remarked, "Life is tough, but it's even tougher when you're stupid." That advice is both hilarious and dead-on accurate. I have learned this truth many times over my forty years. Stupidity is undefeated in its ability to thwart long-term success. I would add to John Wayne's wisdom that life is even tougher when you chase fake rabbits. By failing to seek what truly matters in life, you thwart yourself from attaining authentic happiness – your ultimate goal. We have learned that it does no good to blame others or the popular culture for what we chase. Fake rabbits are indeed all around us and we become enticed when we see others seek money, beauty, and popularity / renown. All of this is imbedded in human nature and unlikely to change any time soon. But now, we have the tools to ignore such meandering and head down a different path. My goal is merely to illuminate that path – you must do all the walking.

Before you embark, I feel compelled to evaluate your progress. This last chapter employs a tool specifically designed for this purpose – a final examination. Just how you wanted this book to end, I know! But fear not, this test contains some profound wisdom. I didn't even come up with the questions; you have Ralph Waldo Emerson to thank. We will take the test and then interpret the results. This chapter concludes with a description of a person who passes the test, a person who is authentically successful … a person who shines!

THE REAL RABBITS FINAL EXAMINATION

This examination is open book, open note, and open everything. You can even ask a friend who knows you well about how you should respond. When was the last time you got to take a test like that? The only requirement is that you must be honest. There is no time limit and you may (and should) take this test again and again. You do not have to pass with flying colors, just be confident that you meet the requirements to answer "Yes" for most of the questions.

When you think about what it means to be authentically happy, you should ponder this beautiful poem by Ralph Waldo Emerson titled SUCCESS. His words sum up my eleven chapters in a mere eight lines. Please read this poem a few times and then answer the questions below.

Success is this:

To laugh often and love much,

*To win the respect of intelligent persons
and the affection of children,*

*To earn the approbation of honest critics and
endure the betrayal of friends,*

To appreciate beauty, to find the best in everything,

*To give of one's self, to leave the world a bit better, whether by a
healthy child, a garden patch, or a redeemed social condition,*

*To have played and laughed with enthusiasm
and to have sung with exultation,*

To know even one life has breathed easier because you have lived.

Each question below comes from a separate part of the poem. Talk about pressure. Each question should be answered "Yes" or "No." A "Maybe" or a "Kind of" should be scored as a "No." Answering in the negative is not necessarily bad as long as you commit to fixing the issue. Here we go:

1. **Do you laugh often and love much?** Before you answer this, ponder how often you laugh each day and whether it is at yourself or others? There is a big difference there. Laughing at yourself is the only answer I accept because that's the only kind of laughter that has proven health benefits. Also, ask whether you take yourself far too seriously. Life is

hard, I know. That's why you must laugh at yourself. A person who rarely laughs is a person likely to hit a brick wall of stress and discontentment.

2. **Do intelligent people respect you?** We all have at least one dopey friend who does dopey things. You can't count that person. What about the intelligent people around you? Do they respect you and what you are all about?

3. **Do little kids and dogs like you?** If yes, you're okay in my book. Kids and dogs have a keen, intuitive sense of identifying and wanting to be around good people.

4. **Do you handle constructive criticism positively?** I ask because this is basically what I have done for the past eleven chapters, dole out constructive criticism. I hope you take my words in the positive spirit in which they are offered.

5. **Do you endure the betrayal of your friends with grace and patience?** Betrayals of friendship are the sad reality of flawed human beings exposing their emotions and interacting closely with each other for long stretches of time. These betrayals are a violation of the implied social contract to be sure. But your reaction to these setbacks matters too. If such a betrayal has not happened to you yet, chances are your time will come. Do you think that you would handle this with grace when it finally happens?

6. **Do you appreciate beauty?** And by beauty, I mean someone's inner beauty, or a colorful sunset, or the sounds and smells of a crisp fall day. Do you take time to appreciate these things on a regular basis?

7. **Do you live your life with the glass half-full?** This is one of my favorite things about teaching freshmen in college – their glasses are always half full. Then, they matriculate to become seniors and their glasses slowly empty. In fact, I rarely meet an adult with a half full glass. How full is yours on a daily basis?

8. **Do you give of yourself (of your time, intelligence, and resources)?** Try and describe your legacy at this stage of life. Is that how you want people to remember you when you are no longer around? Notice also that you can leave a legacy by being a good parent ("a healthy child"),

taking pride in your community ("a garden patch), or curing cancer ("a redeemed social condition"). **This point cannot be overemphasized.** Isn't it wonderful that the impact of each of these three legacies matters equally to authentic happiness! You don't have to cure cancer to make a difference in life.

9. **Do you play with enthusiasm and sing with exultation?** Do you sing in your car? Ralph Waldo Emerson wants you to sing in your car; I'm paraphrasing, of course.

10. **Finally, can you name at least one person whose life is directly better because of you?** For many of us, this is the fuel that gets us up early in the morning. We struggle so that other people (our kids, family, friends, neighbors, or even people we have never met) can rest a little easier. And, we pray that they would do the same for us. Because that's the kind of team I want to be a part of and the type of world I want to live in. How about you?

Have you ever met someone who meets all the criteria of the poem above? Someone who is authentically happy with life? I don't mean the guy you know who makes everybody laugh by picking on others or your sister's friend who is good-looking but completely superficial. I am also not referring to your buddy the genius or your dad's rich friend. Although each of these people may be popular and successful by worldly standards, they are usually not authentically happy.

The type of person that I am talking about is genuinely at peace with life; someone with a small group of amazing friends and a solid character; someone who makes excellent, ethical decisions and takes personal responsibility for vices; someone who has well-aligned priorities – in other words, someone who is authentically successful. Before you spend too much time looking, however, beware that authentically successful people are like the Javan Rhino, the Blue Poison Frog, and the Chinese River Dolphin – extremely rare and difficult to locate. In fact, authentically happy people as a group are beginning to resemble an endangered species.

This is because the road leading towards such a meaningful goal is long and arduous. It is a journey that requires the serious dedication of will, time, and intellect and it will be tough to find many role models to learn from along the way. You will find that the vast majority of people you encounter cannot muster the motivation to do what it takes to be truly happy, don't have a clue what it takes to be truly happy, or just don't care one way or the other. Instead, they sit uncomfortably in the status quo club and, at some point, they give up entirely.

Although I am unable to provide you with all the motivation or the intelligence required for your trek, I have provided a set of detailed directions designed to get you safely to your destination. Think of this book as a roadmap, ever-present and ready to guide you on this important venture. Open it up whenever you need some reassurance, confidence, or even just a smile. Do not be afraid to reread certain pieces of advice or entire sections when you are unsure of what you see in front of you or of the next step to take. Wear out its edges, write all over it, and feel free to e-mail me with questions or comments.

Please remember one more important piece of information. I am not an expert in this area. Just because I created the map does not mean that you will find me waiting for you at the destination. Although I am very content with my life, I still struggle from time to time with many of the concepts described throughout this book. I find myself chasing fake rabbits too and must force myself to refocus my energy and attention on what matters. Therefore, even though we are about to part ways, we will still be headed in the direction of authentic success together.

SHINE FIRST, THEN PAY IT FORWARD

With your final exam in the books and all this information fresh in your head, the ball is now in your court. Chances are you resemble me upon quitting the law firm. This means that you have a great deal of work to do. Fortunately, you are now armed with the tools you need to achieve authentic success. You can either choose to start your journey now or continue to wait for the perfect moment – a perfect moment that will never arrive. Whenever you do choose to venture out, however, make sure to work through the steps in the order you find them here: (1) get on your mark and develop a solid foundation, (2) get set by focusing on contentment, relationships, and character, and (3) align your priorities so can live your life successfully in real-time.

Upon the completion of this journey, something special will happen to you. You will shine. You will be content and happy. Everything about you, from your smile to your character will emanate happiness. This is not a one-time, nirvana moment. You will shine consistently – even on your worst days. Even better, your contentment will be contagious. People will notice something special about your life without you having to say a word. In time, you will begin to receive one of the biggest compliments a human being can receive as people begin to say: "You seem so content and happy with your life. Please tell me why?" Keep in mind that such wonderful compliments are not handed out like candy – you must earn them.

When you finally receive the opportunity to answer such a question, be sure to take the time to tell the story about Cash the greyhound, the false allure of fake rabbits, and the positive ramifications of chasing real rabbits. Always remember that these are the things that allowed you to shine. Now, it is your turn to pay it forward – it is your turn to help others shine as well.

YOUR INFLECTION POINT

This leads us to an inflection point – the place on any curve where the slope changes. You have some choices to make. There are two ways to think about your life at this moment. The first is to consider yourself at the end of an interesting book about success. Here, you feel that all the effort you devoted to the material was time well spent and that you are glad you made it all the way through. You find yourself at the end of something special and it's time to move on and learn about something else. The second way to think about your current state is to consider yourself at the very beginning of your own book about success. Here, you are at the beginning of something special – in this case, a transformed and authentically successful life. I encourage you to choose wisely.

The sport of basketball provides an interesting analogy to describe both, very different, states of mind. At the end of every organized basketball game, a clock inevitably counts down until it reaches 00:00. The moment the last second ticks off, a loud buzzer sounds. This sound is the universal signal for "time is up." At this point, the game is over and everyone stops focusing on the event and heads out – there is nothing else left to see or do. The buzzer represents the end of the line for this experience.

What you may not realize, however, is that the same buzzer that officially ends a basketball game also sounds at the very beginning of each game. When the buzzer sounds, the players come onto the court ready to play and the game officially begins. At this point, the players will need every bit of the practice and preparation undertaken to get them to this place. The starting buzzer serves to focus everyone's attention on the task at hand. Of the two buzzers, it is the starting buzzer that you need to focus on at this very crucial moment in your life. In fact, your newfound dedication to chasing real rabbits places you squarely at the beginning of something very special. You are about to create the life you have always imagined and you will strive to achieve authentic happiness the right way — you will earn it. Therefore, keep your ears open for the starting buzzer because today is where your book begins. The rest is still unwritten.

ACKNOWLEDGMENTS

A significant project of this nature and on this subject must involve other people. I would be nowhere on my journey to authentic success without the efforts of everyone listed below.

Thanks first and foremost to Jillian Ciocchetti – my wonderful wife and best friend. I am truly blessed to have you in my life. You read every word of this book so many times that your head must have spun for weeks. Without your help, this project would be at square one. With you, 2+2 can equal 5. I love my little family. On that note, my daughters–Sophia Grace and Sydney Anne–are the inspiration for most of the things I do in my life these days. Thank you, little ones. I love you … all the time. I want you to grow up and experience authentic happiness just like your daddy!

Special thanks to Marie Calloway, Christina Coughlan, Michelle Kline, Professor Albert Kovacs, and Kathleen Carney for your thoughtful comments and encouragement throughout this process. Earning the respect of my peers is an honor and a privilege.

Thanks to Nicholas Anastasi, Jessica Hunter, Abby Lawes, Jessica Levine, Sydney McLain, Audrey Miklitsch, Alex Shefrin, Rachael Rios, Joshua Stout, Kayla Tadlock, and Bryan Yoshida – my student audience and my friends. Each of you went above and beyond your duty to help me in this endeavor. You already shine in my eyes!

I am grateful to David Hancock, Karen Anderson, and the rest of the staff at Morgan James Publishing for your team's belief in living an authentic life.

A final thanks to my students at the University of Denver over the past twelve years. I truly have found a loophole in life with this career and a lot of that is because of you. Thanks for listening so diligently to my "Professor C's Philosophy on Life" lecture at the end of each academic term and for your valuable comments and insights. Without your encouragement that this topic constituted a worthy subject to write about, I would never have been inspired to convert what was a thirty-minute lecture into an entire book and a national speaking tour. You are the reason why I love coming to work every day and why I have found my calling as a teacher. This book is for you.

ABOUT THE AUTHOR

An Associate Professor of Business Ethics and Legal Studies in the Daniels College of Business at the University of Denver, Corey Ciocchetti is one of the University's most popular and highest-rated professors. Corey joined DU after graduating with a law degree from Duke University School of Law, a Masters degree in Religious Studies and two Bachelors degrees in Finance and Economics—*summa cum laude*—from the University of Denver.

Corey is a talented speaker and teacher and has won multiple teaching and speaking awards including the Outstanding Professor of the Year Award by the University of Denver Alumni Association and the Joel Goldman Award for most respected speaker on the CAMPUSPEAK roster. He currently teaches classes on business law and ethics in a department ranked by the *Wall Street Journal* and *Business Week* in the top ten nationwide for producing students with high ethical standards.

Corey also speaks to tens of thousands of individuals each year about "authentic success" and living an ethical life. He has spoken to diverse audiences, including the University of Hawaii Pediatrics Residency Program, undergraduates at MIT, the Federal Reserve Bank, the National Fire Leadership Academy, the Colorado State Patrol and the third graders of Mapleton School District in Adams County, Colorado (*that one was tough*). He has spoken in over 225 cities and 42 states over the past seven years. A Colorado native, Corey resides in Westminster, Colorado with his wife, Jillian and two daughters, Sophia and Sydney.

Morgan James
Speakers Group

We connect Morgan James published authors with live and online events and audiences whom will benefit from their expertise.